HUMMINGBIRD
GARDENS

Turning Your Yard
Into Hummingbird Heaven

FOR THE ADVANCEMENT OF BOTANY AND THE SERVICE OF THE CITY

BROOKLYN BOTANIC GARDEN PUBLICATIONS ·MM·

Janet Marinelli
SERIES EDITOR

Beth Hanson
CONSULTING EDITOR

Anne Garland
ART DIRECTOR

Mark Tebbitt
SCIENCE EDITOR

Judith D. Zuk
PRESIDENT

Elizabeth Scholtz
DIRECTOR EMERITUS

HUMMINGBIRD GARDENS

Turning Your Yard Into Hummingbird Heaven

Stephen W. Kress-Guest Editor

Steve Buchanan-Illustrator

Handbook #163

Copyright © Summer 2000 by the Brooklyn Botanic Garden, Inc.

Handbooks in the *21st-Century Gardening Series,* formerly *Plants & Gardens,*
are published quarterly at 1000 Washington Ave., Brooklyn, NY 11225.

Subscription included in Brooklyn Botanic Garden subscriber membership dues ($35.00 per year).

ISSN # 0362-5850   ISBN # 1-889538-16-7

Printed by Science Press, a division of the Mack Printing Group.

Printed on recycled paper.

Hummingbirds and their favorite flowers have coevolved over the millennia. The birds use their long bills to probe for nectar at the base of tubular-shaped blooms.

TABLE OF CONTENTS

INTRODUCTION:

"GLITTERING GARMENTS OF THE RAINBOW"

STEPHEN W. KRESS

NEARLY EVERYTHING ABOUT HUMMINGBIRDS is superlative. The common names of many hummers—Ruby-throated, Amethyst-throated, Garnet-throated, Berylline, Crimson-Topaz, and Emerald-chinned—bring to mind their exquisite, gem-like qualities. These tiniest of all vertebrates also have (relative to body size) the largest flight muscles, the biggest brain, the fastest wingbeat, the most rapid heartbeat, the highest body temperature, the greatest appetite, and the most unslakable thirst. Their stamina is so great that they can migrate thousands of miles each year—including hundreds of miles nonstop over water.

Their incessant travels often take hummingbirds to backyard gardens, where they and their insect counterparts, butterflies, congregate. As entrancing as butterflies, hummers dash from one tempting bloom to the next with remarkable energy and agility. It's little wonder that many gardeners are adding hummingbird-attracting blossoms to existing gardens or creating special plantings to lure these feisty visitors. Hummingbirds occasionally visit most gardens, but they only stay when they find special flowers that provide ample food. This handbook explains how you can entice hummingbirds to visit your garden and get them to linger there, enlivening the floral displays with their glittering colors and bold, inquisitive personalities.

If you have already enhanced your yard with special plantings for butterflies, you will note in the pages that follow that gardening for hummingbirds is in many ways similar to gardening for butterflies. For example, both hummingbirds and butterflies share similar tastes in some flowers, such as butterfly weed and gayfeathers. However, one notable

You can attract hummers to your garden by planting their favorite flowers.

difference is that hummingbird flowers are typically red, tube-shaped, and without scent, while butterfly flowers are more varied in color and always heavily perfumed.

Throughout their long migrations, hummingbirds are vulnerable to weather, disease, and predators. Like other migrants, hummingbirds are also vulnerable to habitat loss, pesticides, and collisions with windows, tall buildings, towers, and power lines. There isn't much that gardeners can do to increase the chances of survival of many species of birds, such as those who live deep in forest interiors. By contrast, hummingbirds do profit from backyard plantings where they find meals of nectar and insects, as well as the sugar-water in feeders that sprout from an increasing number of porches and kitchen windows each spring.

Too often, human activities worsen the plight of birds and other wildlife by polluting or destroying their habitats, or through the planting of invasive species that overrun the native vegetation with which wildlife has coevolved. By planting the native wildflowers upon which North American hummingbirds have depended for thousands of years, you will not only bring vibrant color to your garden, but you will also insure a brighter future for the birds that John James Audubon called "glittering garments of the rainbow."

HUMMINGBIRD BIOLOGY
FOR GARDENERS:

LIFESTYLES OF THE
NECTAR SIPPERS

STEPHEN W. KRESS

HUMMINGBIRDS ARE UNIQUE TO THE AMERICAS. The vast majority of the 340 species of hummingbirds occur in the tropics. Twenty-two species are found in the United States, most in the Southwest. Only one species, the Ruby-throated Hummingbird, nests in the eastern states and Canadian provinces.

HUMMINGBIRD MIGRATION

While most hummingbirds are non-migratory or short-distance migrants, there are two notable exceptions. The Rufous Hummingbird migrates from its winter home in Mexico as far north as southern Alaska. Remarkably, many Ruby-throated Hummingbirds migrate more than 600 miles across the Gulf of Mexico, making landfall in the southeastern states. After crossing the border, some continue north, while others move eastward, reoccupying nesting habitat in all the eastern states and Canadian provinces.

NECTAR SIPPING

The appearance of migrating hummingbirds in spring may be timed to the appearance of nectar-producing wildflowers—or perhaps the flowers time their blooming to the arrival of the hummingbirds! For example, arrival of the Ruby-throated Hummingbird in the northern part of its range, where it nests, coincides with the flowering of certain nectar plants such as wild columbine (*Aquilegia canadensis*), as well as with the arrival of migrating Yellow-bellied Sapsuckers, which provide "sap wells" from which hummingbirds readily feed. Hummingbirds of the western moun-

The Rufous Hummingbird migrates from its winter home in Mexico as far north as Alaska.

tains also appear to time their migration to coincide with the flowering of favorite nectar plants. (Hummingbirds' southern migration in autumn is triggered by changes in day length, not by the scarcity of nectar plants, which are still abundant.)

While many birds, including orioles and at least 50 other species, have an appetite for sugar-water and tree sap, hummingbirds are the ultimate nectar specialists. This high-energy diet provides ample fuel for flight speeds of 66 miles per hour—and up to 200 wing strokes per second—during courtship. Ruby-throated Hummingbirds typically weigh less than 4 grams (females are slightly heavier), but their body weight can double in a week as they fatten on nectar, as well as insects and spiders, before beginning their fall migration.

FLEXIBLE FLYING

Hummingbirds are the only birds that can fly up, down, sideways, and even backward, a talent that enables them to easily sip nectar from flowers and pluck invertebrates out of thin air. Such extraordinary flight is due in part to their relatively huge breast muscles, which comprise up to 30 percent of their total weight—the highest proportion of any bird.

Their fast-paced foraging style permits hummingbirds to hover where there are no convenient perches—for instance, at the entrance to swaying

While many birds have an appetite for sugar-water and tree sap, hummingbirds are the ultimate flower nectar specialists.

flower stems, where they feed in place. This unique hovering ability permits them to feed on as many as 1,500 flowers each day; they may drink twice their weight in sugar-water daily. Their skill at backward flight allows them to back off to look over the banquet scene before charging forward for refueling.

BODY HEAT

Relative to their body size, hummingbirds have the largest heart of all warm-blooded animals, with the fastest heartbeat—1,260 beats each minute. Their daytime body temperature reaches 105 degrees F. Hummers are the only birds that regularly become torpid at night, when their temperature plummets from daytime levels.

HUMMINGBIRD IQ

Although hummingbirds are curious and are often attracted to bright red colors on objects that have little resemblance to flowers (such as colorful clothing and red stripes on flags), they quickly learn which red objects provide productive treats. They also have remarkable memories and can recall from one year to the next the location of a particularly rich nectar patch or reliable hummingbird feeder. Observations of partially albino birds (which have unique color patterns) have demonstrated that individual hummingbirds often return to the same backyard over several consecutive years, which may be most of their relatively short lives.

FITTING THE BILL

Hummingbirds and their favorite flowers have clearly coevolved for mutual benefit. Most hummingbird flowers have a recognizable shape, regardless of their family affinities. Look for tubular-shaped flowers with stamens and pistil often dangling from the flower's entrance. The typical flower shape protects a nectar bait that encourages these long-billed birds to probe deep for their sweet meal. In the process, birds pick up pollen on their crown, and the pollen is then transferred to the next flower from which the birds feed. Some hummingbirds have learned to "steal" nectar by piercing the side of the flower without picking up pollen, but plants such as bird-of-paradise and other heliconias have evolved to counter this behavior with a thickened calyx that discourages nectar thieves.

Many hummingbird-pollinated plants have red or orange flowers, colors that are readily seen by hummingbirds. Unlike insect-pollinated flowers, hummingbird-pollinated blooms are usually not fragrantly perfumed, because hummingbirds (like most birds) have a poorly developed sense of smell.

BUSIER THAN BEES

Compared to insect pollinators such as bees, hummingbirds offer distinct advantages as cross-pollinators. Bees are inactive in cool, wet weather and visit flowers only during the warmer part of the day when their wing muscles have adequately warmed for flight. Hummingbirds are generally better pollinators than bees because they must feed continuously from dawn to dusk. In addition, bees' activities are more confined to fields and forest edges, and they seldom visit forest interiors, as hummingbirds do. One study that compared the pollinating efficiency of Ruby-throated Hummingbirds and bumblebees found that hummingbirds deposited ten times as much pollen (per stigma per visit) onto the flowers of the trumpet flower, or trumpet creeper, *Campsis radicans*. Another study found that closely related species such as bee balm, *Monarda didyma* and *M. clinopodia,* may avoid hybridization because particular hummingbird species show preferences for certain nectar flavors and pollen is placed on the hummers in slightly different locations.

COURTSHIP RITUALS

The hummingbird nesting season begins when the male establishes a courtship territory. When a female enters the territory, the male per-

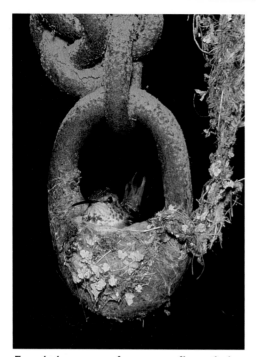

Female hummers often camouflage their nests with lichens.

forms a courtship flight unique to his species. In Ruby-throated Hummingbirds, this is a looping, U-shaped flight performed as high as 36 to 45 feet above the female. If impressed by the skill of his flight, the female lands near the male, encouraging him to shift the performance to a series of very fast, close, side-to-side horizontal arcs, which he performs (with throat gorget extended) within one to two feet of the female. Mating soon follows the courtship performance.

NESTING

Females build their nests by themselves on a shrub or tree branch, using mainly thistle and dandelion down. The nest is secured to the branch with spider web and pine resin; its exterior is sometimes camouflaged with lichens, held in place by sticky spider web. Construction takes six to ten days, and during this time, the male continues courting additional mates. Females sometimes refurbish old nests for a second brood, or they may build another nest for their second brood while still feeding the first brood.

A female usually lays two tiny white eggs and incubates them for 12 to 14 days. She broods the young almost constantly until they are nine days old, leaving her nest and young only to obtain food for herself and her brood. Nestlings are fully feathered and capable of flight when they are 18 to 20 days old.

PREDATORS

Hummingbirds have few predators, but shrikes, American Kestrels, and Sharp-shinned Hawks sometimes take adults, and Blue Jays will take eggs. Attacks by praying mantises, dragonflies, and bullfrogs have also been documented, and hummingbirds are sometimes accidentally entangled in spider webs. House cats are probably the most common predators, and collisions with windows, cars, and radio towers are believed to take a huge toll on hummingbird populations.

HUMMINGBIRDS
OF NORTH AMERICA

LYNN HASSLER KAUFMAN

This encyclopedia includes the 18 species of hummingbirds found in the United States and Canada, as well as four "accidentals"—species that are very rarely seen this far north. The encyclopedia entry for each bird includes information on its native range, preferred habitats, and nesting habits, as well as tips to aid in identification. Please note that the hummingbird illustrations are not drawn to scale; see the information in each entry on length (measured from tip of bill to tip of tail) for the accurate size of each species. See the Encyclopedia of Hummingbird Plants, beginning on page 49, for detailed descriptions of hummingbird-attracting flowers for every region.

ALLEN'S HUMMINGBIRD
Selasphorus sasin

Allen's Hummingbird is one of the two common nesting hummingbirds in northern California gardens. The genus name *Selasphorus* means "flame bearing" in Latin. Allen's like to feed on red tubular flowers such as penstemon, monkeyflower, and paintbrush.

RANGE Nests from southwestern Oregon to southwestern California; winters in Mexico. Non-migratory race on the Channel Islands and Palos Verdes Peninsula in southern California

HABITAT Coastal mountain meadows, wooded canyons, as well as city gardens near the coast

MIGRATION In late winter moves north up the Pacific Coast from Mexico. Some individuals go south through mountains in late summer.

IDENTIFICATION 3 inches long. Male has metallic green back, reddish brown sides, rump, tail, and cheeks. Throat is bright reddish orange. Females and young birds almost impossible to separate from Rufous in the field.

NESTING HABITS Nests in tree or shrub on horizontal or diagonal branch up to 90 feet above the ground. Sometimes nests in pines, or even in buildings; usually in dense shade.

ANNA'S HUMMINGBIRD
Calypte anna

More vocal than most hummers, the male Anna's has a rather unmelodic song: a series of repetitive scratchy notes, often delivered while perched. In winter Anna's often feeds at eucalyptus and tree tobacco flowers.

♂

♀

RANGE Very common, Pacific Coast north to British Columbia, east to Arizona

HABITAT Suburban gardens, coastal sage scrub, oak woodland, city parks

MIGRATION Southwestern birds migrate east to west. Arizona birds fly west to California in mid-spring and return in later summer.

IDENTIFICATION 4 inches long; chunky with bright metallic green back and gray underparts. Male has a rose-red crown and throat. Females are plainer but they usually show a small patch of color on the throat.

NESTING HABITS Some birds begin nesting in December; sites include branches of shrubs and trees (often in oaks), 17 to 30 feet up. Female builds nest out of plant fibers and spider webs, often camouflaged on the outside with lichen.

BERYLLINE HUMMINGBIRD
Amazilia beryllina

This hummingbird has been a rare but regular visitor to the U.S. since 1964. When it does show up, it tends to stick around for several months at a time. Berylline feeds at thistles and will frequent feeders. Its three-noted song sounds like a tiny trumpet.

RANGE Uplands of Mexico; regular visitor in summer to mountains of southeastern Arizona

HABITAT Shady canyons, among sycamores, or open pine-oak woodland in Arizona, at 5,000 to 7,000 feet. Foothills and lower slopes of mountains in Mexico, especially in oak woodland

MIGRATION Probably not migratory over most of its range. In parts of Mexico may move to lower elevations for winter. In summer strays north into southwestern U.S.

IDENTIFICATION 4 inches long; sexes similar. Head and body mostly glittering green, rufous in wings, rump, and tail. Bill black with some red. Female slightly duller, with gray belly.

NESTING HABITS 17 to 25 feet above ground on horizontal branch. In Arizona usually nests in sycamores.

BLACK-CHINNED HUMMINGBIRD
Archilochus alexandri

This species is named for the male, which has a black chin or throat. Black-chinneds often repeatedly flick their tails while hovering over flowers.

RANGE Widespread at low elevations in the West; summers from British Columbia to central Texas and Southern California, winters in Mexico

HABITAT Semi-open arid lowlands, suburbs, open woods, parks, gardens, riparian woodland

MIGRATION Strictly migratory. Arrives in western U.S. in spring and leaves for Mexico in fall. Small numbers may stray east in fall, and a few may winter near the Gulf Coast.

IDENTIFICATION 3 inches long; underparts whitish. Male is bright metallic green above, has a black throat with white collar below. In certain lights the throat shows an iridescent purple border. Females and young birds may have dusky streaks on throat.

NESTING HABITS Usually nests on a horizontal or diagonal branch in a deciduous tree or shrub 4 to 8 feet up. Often nests in backyards and gardens.

BLUE-THROATED HUMMINGBIRD
Lampornis clemenciae

The largest of the U.S.-breeding hummingbirds, Blue-throats are the size of some sparrows. As they approach other hummers at flowers or feeders, they aggressively flash their striking black and white tails. Blue-throats like shady spots near water. Their call note is a squeaky "seek," often delivered in flight.

♂

♀

RANGE Southwestern U.S. to southern Mexico

HABITAT Wooded streams in lower mountain canyons, sycamores, pine-oak woodland, coniferous forest

MIGRATION Most U.S. birds depart in fall; probably resident over most of its range in Mexico.

IDENTIFICATION 5 inches long. Green above; large black tail with white corners, two white face stripes. Male has light blue throat, often difficult to see, and gray underparts. Female's throat is gray.

NESTING HABITS Usually streamside on branch sheltered by overhanging limb, sometimes on exposed root on undercut stream bank or under building eaves; 1 to 30 feet up. Outer covering of nest is green moss, unique among North American hummer nests.

BROAD-BILLED HUMMINGBIRD
Cynanthus latirostris

Broad-bills have a limited range in the U.S., but are abundant where found. Their distinctive voice is a series of dry, crackling notes.

RANGE March to September in limited areas of Arizona, New Mexico, and southwest Texas; winters in Mexico

HABITAT Desert canyons, low oak woodlands, foothills, and streamsides with sycamores or cottonwoods, mesquite thickets

MIGRATION Spring through summer nests in the Southwest; migrates south into Mexico in the fall. Small numbers may overwinter in Arizona and southern California.

IDENTIFICATION 4 inches long; male glistens all over with iridescent feathers of green and blue, including metallic blue throat; reddish orange bill; forked tail is blackish blue. Female has grayish under-parts, eye stripe, reddish bill, and blackish blue tail.

♂

NESTING HABITS Deciduous shrub, vine, or low branch on tree 3 to 9 feet above ground. Unlike most other North American hummers, does not usually use lichen on outside of nest.

♀

BROAD-TAILED HUMMINGBIRD
Selasphorus platycercus

This is the classic hummingbird of the mountain West. Adult male broad-tails create high-pitched trilling sounds with certain wing feathers while flying.

RANGE Breeds in south and central Rockies and mountains of the Great Basin south into western Texas and Mexico; winters in Mexico to Guatemala

HABITAT Mountain meadows and forests to over 10,000 feet

MIGRATION Adult males usually migrate before females and young. Broad-tails tend to fly northward through lowlands in the spring, and south through the mountains in late summer.

IDENTIFICATION 4 inches long; males have bronze-green backs and bright rose-pink throats. Females and young birds are whitish underneath with some reddish brown on flanks and at sides of tail.

NESTING HABITS Nests on low horizontal branches of willow, alder, pine, fir, spruce, aspen; sheltered from above by overhanging branch, 4 to 15 feet up. Males often launch from willow thickets in mountain meadows for their display flights.

BUFF-BELLIED HUMMINGBIRD
Amazilia yucatanensis

Buff-bellied Hummingbirds are part of the tropical element in south Texas, often seen visiting flowers such as Turk's cap, red salvia, and red yucca.

RANGE Resident in Mexico, Belize, and Guatemala; mostly summer resident in south Texas

HABITAT Woodland edges, areas of brush and scattered trees, suburban neighborhoods, especially those with extensive gardens

MIGRATION Relatively common in southern Texas in summer; some individuals remain through the winter. A few move north along coast in fall and winter to upper Texas coast and Louisiana.

IDENTIFICATION 4 inches long; bronzy green back with chestnut tail; throat and breast shiny emerald green; lower breast and belly cinnamon buff. Both sexes look similar.

NESTING HABITS Usually nests in large shrub or small tree such as hackberry, Texas ebony, or cordia. Nest is low, 3 to 10 feet off ground on horizontal or drooping branch or in fork of twig. May refurbish or build on top of old nests.

CALLIOPE HUMMINGBIRD
Stellula calliope

This tiny bird is the smallest in North America. Despite its small size, it is able to survive cold summer nights at high elevations in the Rockies. It is the only U.S. hummer with such a distinctive throat patch. *Stellula* in Latin means "little star."

RANGE Summers in mountains of western North America from southwest Canada to Baja; winters in Mexico

HABITAT High mountain forests and meadows; pine-oak woods in Mexico

MIGRATION Migrates northwest in early spring through Pacific lowlands, southeast in late summer mostly through Rocky Mountain region.

IDENTIFICATION 3 inches long; short bill and tail. Male green above, white below, greenish sides. Reddish purple on throat forms streaks. Female green above, underside tinged with buff; throat lightly spotted.

NESTING HABITS Nests almost to timberline, 10,000 to 11,500 feet. Site is on twig or branch under overhanging foliage, usually 6 to 40 feet up. Sometimes builds on base of old pine cone, making nest look like part of the cone.

COSTA'S HUMMINGBIRD
Calypte costae

The male Costa's performs a daring aerial courtship display. He rises high in the air, often 100 feet or more, and then plunges downward, making a shrill continuous whistle. At the bottom of his dive, he pulls up sharply and flies upward again.

RANGE Deserts of southwestern U.S. (mainly Arizona and California) and northwestern Mexico

HABITAT Desert washes, sage scrub, lower parts of dry canyons among cacti, yucca, and ocotillo

MIGRATION Many of the birds that nest in the desert in spring migrate west to the coast for other seasons.

IDENTIFICATION 3 inches long; male has iridescent violet crown and violet throat that sweeps back to a sharp point and flares out on either side of his neck. Female has a green back; crown often dull brown; dingy white below.

NESTING HABITS Nests in open spots with good visibility, sparsely leafed shrubs or small trees, 2 to 8 feet up; often in yucca. In some areas has adapted to nesting in suburbs.

GREEN VIOLETEAR
Colibri thalassinus

This hummingbird is widespread in the mountains of the tropics. Males often perch high in trees and endlessly sing a monotonous series of dry notes. One or two wander into Texas almost every year, and the species has strayed as far east as North Carolina and as far north as Canada.

RANGE Highlands of Mexico south to Bolivia

HABITAT Oak woods and clearings; forest edges

MIGRATION Nomadic; does not have known regular migration, but ranges far and wide.

IDENTIFICATION 4 inches long; appears dark green overall. Bill slightly downward curving. Male has violet-blue ear patches and breast. Female similar but duller; breast patch smaller or absent.

NESTING HABITS Down and moss cup nest, often placed low.

LUCIFER HUMMINGBIRD
Calothorax lucifer

Lucifer Hummingbird is typical of the Chihuahuan Desert of central Mexico, where it frequents flowering agave stalks and ocotillo. A few reach the southwestern U.S.

RANGE West Texas to southern Mexico; locally in southeast Arizona and southwest New Mexico

HABITAT Arid slopes, agaves, desert canyons

MIGRATION Migratory in northern part of range. Birds from southwest U.S. and northern Mexico winter in plateaus of south-central Mexico.

IDENTIFICATION 3 inches long; bronzy green back; long decurved bill. Male has dazzling purple throat and sides of neck, buffy sides, and long forked tail that is usually tightly folded. Female's breast uniformly buff colored; pale streak behind eye.

NESTING HABITS Male has a unique courtship display performed in front of female at her nest. Makes short flights back and forth with loud rustling sound of wings, then flies high and dives steeply past the nest. Site is in open cholla cactus, on an ocotillo stem, or agave stalk, 2 to 10 feet up.

MAGNIFICENT HUMMINGBIRD
Eugenes fulgens

At a distance, this very large hummingbird looks all black. Its wingbeats are slower than those of smaller hummingbirds and are actually discernible in flight. *Fulgens* is from the Latin "fulgere," meaning to gleam or glitter. Formerly called Rivoli's Hummingbird.

RANGE Southwestern U.S to Panama; strays have been seen as far north as Minnesota

HABITAT Pine-oak woodlands, canyons with sycamore, and coniferous forests in higher mountains, 5,000 to 9,000 feet

MIGRATION Southwest U.S. residents probably migrate only a short distance south into Mexico for the winter. Occasionally a few will winter at feeders in canyons of Arizona.

IDENTIFICATION 5 inches long; male has dark belly, bright emerald-green throat and purple crown. Female is green above, dusky green below, with a spotted throat and subtle pale tail corners.

NESTING HABITS 10 to 60 feet above ground on a horizontal branch in open area of a tree such as pine or maple.

RUBY-THROATED HUMMINGBIRD
Archilochus colubris

Ruby-throated is the only hummingbird found regularly east of the Great Plains. In its northern distribution it often feeds on tree sap provided by the drilling of sapsuckers. It is especially attracted to flowers of bee balm, trumpet creeper, columbine, and red salvia.

RANGE Southeastern Canada to Gulf states; winters south Texas, south Florida to western Panama

HABITAT Gardens, woodland edges, city parks; winters in open or dry tropical scrub

MIGRATION Many migrate around the Gulf of Mexico, but others may fly across it—600 miles over open water.

IDENTIFICATION 3 inches long; iridescent green back, forked tail. Undersides whitish, sides and flanks dusky green. Male has a fiery red throat. Female throat whitish, grayish white below with slightly buffy sides

NESTING HABITS On horizontal branch or one that slopes downward in deciduous tree such as maple or beech, or hemlock; also in large shrubs. May reuse old nests.

RUFOUS HUMMINGBIRD
Selasphorus rufus

Feisty and aggressive, Rufous Hummingbirds defend patches of flowers or feeders, driving away other birds that attempt to approach. This bird is a champion long-distance migrant, wintering in Mexico and nesting as far north as Alaska—farther north than any other hummer.

RANGE Pacific Northwest to south central Alaska; winters in Mexico; small numbers winter in Gulf Coast states

HABITAT Forest edges and clearings, streamsides

MIGRATION In spring moves northward through Pacific lowlands. Beginning in late June, moves southeast through Rocky Mountains and Sierra, following seasonal blooming of flowers.

IDENTIFICATION 3 inches long; male has brilliant reddish brown back with flaming orange-red throat. Females and young birds have rufous on tail and sides and are indistinguishable from Allen's.

NESTING HABITS Courtship display by male is a steep U or vertical oval; makes whining and popping sounds at bottom of dive. Nest is usually well hidden in lower part of coniferous trees, deciduous shrubs or vines, 3 to 30 feet up.

PLAIN-CAPPED STARTHROAT
Heliomaster constantii

This large, drab hummingbird is a rare visitor to southern Arizona. In its native habitat it is often seen hovering over rivers catching insects.

RANGE Mexico and Central America

HABITAT Dry thorn forests; in Arizona has been found in lowland areas near streams or open, lower parts of canyons

MIGRATION Probably doesn't migrate within permanent range; has reached Arizona mostly in summer and fall.

IDENTIFICATION 4 inches long; overall looks quite dull; long billed. Male has red throat but color is quite difficult to see; white stripes on face; white rump and tufts on flanks.

NESTING HABITS Cup-shaped nest in branches of trees and shrubs.

VIOLET-CROWNED HUMMINGBIRD
Amazilia violiceps

This hummingbird only recently arrived in the U.S. It was unknown north of the border until the late 1950s and is still quite scarce and localized. Where flowers are not abundant, it can be seen hovering mid-level in the shade of tall trees, catching insects.

RANGE Mainly western Mexico; regular in summer in a few places in southeast Arizona and southwest New Mexico

HABITAT Arid or semiarid open woodland; in U.S. mostly near groves of tall trees (especially sycamores and cottonwoods) with brushy understory

MIGRATION Probably permanent resident over most of range; but in U.S., is seen mostly in summer.

IDENTIFICATION 4 inches long; sexes similar; bright white underparts including the throat. Bill bright red, tipped with black. Upperparts bronzy green, tail greenish. Violet-blue crown, duller in female.

NESTING HABITS Squeaky song often heard at dawn during breeding season. Favors deciduous trees, especially sycamore, or large shrub in open but shaded spot 4 to 40 feet up.

WHITE-EARED HUMMINGBIRD
Hylocharis leucotis

This Mexican species is a regular but uncommon visitor to the mountain forests of southeastern Arizona.

RANGE Mexican border to Nicaragua; a few reach southwestern U.S.

HABITATS In Mexico, high mountain forests; in clearings and edges of coniferous forests; pine-oak woods at middle elevations. In southern Arizona most are seen in mountain canyons where feeders are maintained.

MIGRATION Probably permanent resident over most of range. Strays north of Mexico in summer; has wintered at feeders in Arizona.

IDENTIFICATION 3 inches long; sports a bright red bill tipped with black; blackish blue forked tail, long white stripe behind eye. Male has blue and green throat and purple crown. Female has white stripe behind eye and small green spots on throat.

NESTING HABITS Males gather in loose groups, perch 60 to 100 feet apart, and sing short songs to attract females. Nest site is 5 to 20 feet above ground on a twig or in fork of shrub or tree.

RARE VISITORS

Green-breasted Mango

The following "accidental" species are very rare visitors to the United States.

GREEN-BREASTED MANGO
Anthracothorax prevostii

This large, bulky hummer with a slightly curved bill is widespread in the lowlands of the American tropics around forest edges and clearings. It has wandered to southern Texas a few times. Male is all green (blacker on throat) with a magenta tail. Female has a wide black stripe down the center of the white breast.

BAHAMA WOODSTAR
Calliphlox evelynae

Native to islands in the Bahamas, but occasionally wanders to southern Florida. The male is green above with a deeply forked black and buffy tail. A white upper breast band, like a partial collar, contrasts with cinnamon belly and purple throat. Female has a white throat and unforked tail.

XANTUS'S HUMMINGBIRD
Hylocharis xantusii

Specialty of the southern half of Baja California; likes mountain canyons, especially with water. Has been found very rarely in southern California and once in British Columbia. Males have emerald-green throats, black-tipped reddish bills, and a white stripe behind the eye. The underparts are mainly buffy and the tail is chestnut colored.

Female Xantus's are all buff below, with chestnut in the tail.

CINNAMON
HUMMINGBIRD
Amazilia rutila

A common, colorful hummer of arid scrub and brushy forest edges in western and southern Mexico. It was not recorded in the U.S. until 1992, when one was found in southern Arizona. Both sexes have green backs and bright cinnamon underparts. The tail is rufous and the bill is red tipped with black.

Above: Cinnamon Hummingbird
Below: Xantus's Hummingbird

HUMMINGBIRD MOTHS:

MARVELOUS MASQUERADERS

STEPHEN W. KRESS

HUMMINGBIRD GARDENS ARE IDEAL PLACES to watch for hummer look-alikes—the hummingbird moths. In a classic example of convergent evolution, these swept-winged, stout-bodied insects dine on flower nectar and pollinate flowers in a manner remarkably similar to hummingbirds. Like their avian namesakes, they can hover seemingly motionless, while tapping nectar reserves with their long, coiled tongue. Some species even have green backs, further adding to their hummingbird resemblance. Unlike hummingbirds, though, they are late risers, waiting until the sun warms their wing muscles to stir them into action.

Members of the sphinx moth family, this enormously varied group derives its family name from the caterpillars that can pull their forebody up into a sphinx-like pose. The caterpillars are known as hornworms because they have a long, harmless spine that arises menacingly from their back near their posterior. While most sphinx moths visit flowers at night, hummingbird moths (also called clearwings because of the transparent patches in their wings) frequent gardens in full daylight. At a distance, some black and yellow species resemble huge bumblebees; however, bees settle on the flower, descending into the bloom, while hummingbird moths feed in a tireless manner, seldom resting.

Hummingbird-moth caterpillars feed mainly on honeysuckle, hawthorn, snowberry, and viburnum, but different species have special taste preferences. The caterpillars transform into pupae, which are enclosed in well-hidden, dense brown cocoons formed on the ground under fallen leaves. Some pupae overwinter under leaves, transforming themselves into flying adults the following spring. Double- or triple-brooded species pass through the pupal stage in midsummer, emerging as adults in late summer and fall.

Taxonomists have struggled with this group, since the different

Hummingbird moths, like their avian namesakes, can hover seemingly motionless while drinking flower nectar with their long, coiled tongues.

species vary in appearance at different locations in their vast ranges, and even different broods in the same location may look somewhat different. It is now generally agreed, however, that there are four species of hummingbird moths in North America. Range can help to sort them out, but several species overlap and at first glance they look similar. All species have clear parts in their wings and the males have a dramatic anal tuft, often in varied colors. In northern climates, hummingbird moths appear in midsummer, while those in southern climates often have two broods, the first in midspring, the second in midsummer into late fall.

Hummingbird gardeners don't have to plant special flowers to attract the adults, but the larvae do require specific shrubs for food (see species write-ups that follow). Here are some tips for recognizing the four species:

COMMON CLEARWING
Hemaris thysbe

This is the largest and most common of the hummingbird moths. Although there is considerable variation, the abdomen is marked with narrow or broad bands. The thorax is generally uniform muddy yellow or solid brown. As is the case in other hummingbird moths, the forewings have clear cells edged with black. Males have a distinctive black tuft at the tip of their abdomen.

RANGE Newfoundland to Florida, across to Texas, north along the eastern Great Plains, west to southern British Columbia, then north to southern Alaska

SEASONS In the north, this species has one brood and adults occur in midsummer. In the South, where two broods are produced, adults visit gardens from March to June and again from August to October.

CATERPILLAR FOODS Hawthorns *(Crataegus* species), cherries and plums *(Prunus* species), honeysuckles *(Lonicera* species), and snowberry *(Symphoricarpos* species)

GRACEFUL CLEARWING
Hemaris gracilis

This is the least common of the four species, but it may be locally abundant, especially in the mid-Atlantic states. It closely resembles the common clearwing, but is easily distinguished by the pair of red-brown bands on the sides of its thorax. The thorax varies from green to yellow-green and sometimes brown. The underside of the thorax is white. The abdomen is pale red with three rows of white spots on the underside. The anal tuft is black, divided in the middle with reddish hairs. Specimens from South Carolina and Florida are usually dark brown.

RANGE Nova Scotia to central Florida along the East Coast and west through the New England states to Michigan

SEASONS In the northern part of its range, it may have two broods or have a long emergence period. Adults start feeding at flowers in Nova Scotia from early June to early August; Michigan from the end of May through early July; New York in mid-May and July; South Carolina in April; and central Florida in late March.

CATERPILLAR FOODS Unknown

SNOWBERRY CLEARWING
Hemaris diffinis

This is a variable species, with more black markings on the thorax, abdomen, and legs than other clearwings.

RANGE Nova Scotia to Florida across to California and north to British Columbia and the Northwest Territories

SEASONS This species has two broods throughout most of its range. Adults begin visiting flowers from spring into midsummer.

CATERPILLAR FOODS Various species of dogbane *(Apocynum)*, dwarf bush honeysuckle *(Diervilla lonicera)*, snowberries *(Symphoricarpos* species) and honeysuckles *(Lonicera* species)

CALIFORNIA CLEARWING
Hemaris senta

The head, thorax, and basal segments of the abdomen are brownish olive or olive-green. The abdomen is black or olive-green above and yellow below, except for a broad yellow band just above the terminal segment of the abdomen. The anal tuft is completely black. The wings have a very narrow border of brown, and the clear parts of the wings have a steel-blue luster in certain light. Sometimes the wings are pale rusty red above and below where they insert into the thorax.

RANGE New Mexico, Colorado, Utah, Wyoming, west to California and British Columbia

SEASONS Adults are on the wing May to mid August.

CATERPILLAR FOODS Unknown

15 WAYS TO KEEP THEM COMING

STEPHEN W. KRESS

HUMMINGBIRDS PREFER OPENINGS IN THE FOREST and forest edge, and so are readily drawn to suburban and rural gardens that offer a mix of tall trees, shrubs, and patches of meadow and lawn. They are less likely to frequent cities, perhaps because they find fewer flowering plants for food and trees for nesting. Yet even in the largest cities, hummingbirds occupy parks and sometimes visit window boxes or rooftop gardens planted with bright flowers, especially during migration.

Once hummingbirds discover your property, the same individuals are likely to return each year at about the same time; they are remarkable creatures of habit. The number of hummingbirds that frequent your yard is closely linked to the abundance of food, water, nesting sites, and perches. Following are 15 practical steps you can take to create an ideal hummingbird garden.

STEP 1

Draw a sketch of your yard, indicating the location of the house and outbuildings such as garages and tool sheds. Include trees, shrubs, existing flower beds, and other features likely to benefit hummingbirds. Work with these existing features, enhancing them with additional plantings.

STEP 2

Using your landscape sketch, find a good spot to be the focus of your

Right: Keep in mind that hummingbirds are attracted to red, pink, and orange tubular-shaped flowers such as this *Ipomopsis rubra*.

Hummingbird gardens needn't be large—even a window box or hanging planter will do.

hummingbird garden. A site near a window or patio door will give you a front seat on the action. Hummingbird gardens need not be large—even a flower box or trellis will do. Gardens planted exclusively with hummingbird plants will attract more birds, but even a few choice plants added to existing gardens will feed some hummers.

STEP 3

Think vertically when planning your hummingbird garden. Use trellises, trees, garden sheds, or other structures to support climbing vines; add window boxes, wooden tubs, or ceramic pots to create a terraced effect and provide growing places for a variety of plants.

STEP 4

Select native plants for your garden. Learn which plants hummingbirds feed on in natural areas near your home. Native hummingbird plants and local hummingbird species have a long association in which plants serve as a reliable source of nectar at the same time each year. Keep in mind that cultivated varieties of impatiens and rhododendrons may look promising, but have little value to hummingbirds; these are selected for flower size, color, and shape, but are not good nectar producers. Do not plant exotic flowering plants, such as Japanese and tartarian honeysuckles, which are attractive to

Hummers usually line their nests with soft fibers, so include some fuzzy plants in your garden.

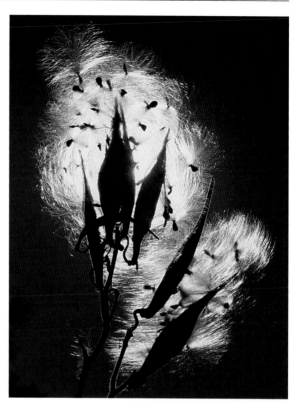

hummingbirds but invade neighboring fields and woodlands, crowding out more beneficial native shrubs and wildflowers.

STEP 5

Choose red, tubular flowers, as these are quick clues to a flower's value as a hummingbird food supply. Hummingbirds are also attracted to orange and pink flowers, but they find yellow and white blooms less attractive. Red, non-tubular flowers such as roses and geraniums may lure hummingbirds with their blooms, but they offer little nectar, so the birds quickly reject them. Flowers that rely on sweet scents to attract insect pollinators usually do not provide a nectar source for hummingbirds.

STEP 6

Plant patches of the same species (three or more plants) to provide larger quantities of nectar.

STEP 7

Select plants that bloom at different times of the year to provide nectar throughout the hummingbird season.

STEP 8

Prune your plants to prevent excessive woody growth and instead favor production of flowers.

STEP 9

Learn about local hummingbird habits and which species are likely to occur near your home. Study the migration dates, nesting season, and seasonal presence. This knowledge will help you select plants that will bloom during the time that hummingbirds are likely to visit your yard.

STEP 10

Include some fuzzy plants. Hummingbirds usually line their nest with soft plant fibers. Two favorites are cinnamon fern, which has a fuzzy stem, and pussy willow. Leave some thistle and dandelion, other favorite nest-building materials, in your yard.

STEP 11

Provide water baths. Like most birds, hummingbirds frequently bathe in shallow water—even in the drops that collect on leaves. Hummingbirds may sit and fluff and preen or flit through the droplets generated by garden misters, drip fountain devices, and small waterfalls; these are available at many garden shops.

The small waterfall and the bright red blooms of bee balm make this garden a more enticing spot for hummingbirds.

STEP 12

If your garden does not include trees or shrubs and there are none nearby, position perches within 10 to 20 feet of the garden. As a substitute for a live perch, use a dead branch with small twigs (keep in mind the tiny size of hummingbird toes).

STEP 13

Large trees are often used for perches, as springboards for courtship displays, and for nesting. The trunks of large trees also provide hummingbirds a source of lichens—a camouflaging decoration that some species attach to the outsides of their nests with spider silk. If space permits, plant a large tree such as a maple or oak. If you have a smaller yard, plant smaller trees that can provide nest sites and serve as food sources.

Hummers are fond of small branches on which they can perch.

STEP 14

Be persistent. Hummingbirds may appear minutes after you set out inviting plants, but sometimes it takes several weeks before they chance on your garden. Even with luscious red flowers as bait, pure chance may keep your feeder a secret until the first migrant discovers it. Once hummingbirds do start visiting your garden, they are likely to continue throughout the season and will usually return the following year. If visits drop off for a week or two in midsummer, the reason may be that an especially attractive nearby flower patch may have temporarily diverted your hummingbirds.

STEP 15

Avoid insecticides. Hummingbirds can ingest poisons when they eat insects; systemic herbicides can also be found in flower nectar.

HUMMINGBIRD FEEDERS

STEPHEN W. KRESS

T HE BEST WAY TO FEED HUMMINGBIRDS is to offer them nectar-producing flowers, but hummingbird feeders can act as a supplement and lure birds to spots where you can easily watch them. Hummingbirds are entranced by sugar-water in colorful feeders—after all, no flower in nature has such vast amounts of sweet nectar. Yet hummingbird feeders can become hazards to the birds unless they are responsibly tended. Here are a few suggestions:

When you purchase your first hummingbird feeder, choose one with a small reservoir for sugar-water. You will have to fill this more frequently, but the sugar-water supply will be fresher. As hummingbirds find your feeder and make it a popular stop, add more feeders or a larger feeder, selecting models that are easy to clean. Feeders with multiple sipping ports and perches can accommodate many birds at once.

Hang the feeder in a shady spot; the sugar water is less likely to spoil there. Keep the feeder within easy view of windows; placing the feeder within a foot or two of a window is usually safe, but move it if hummingbirds begin colliding with the glass. Also keep the feeder at least six feet off the ground to reduce the risk from predatory house cats. Place the feeder near a shrub or tree, which can provide convenient, nearby perches and shelter—or securely nail a branch with tiny branchlets close by to accommodate hummingbird feet.

To attract hummingbirds when you first put up the feeder, dangle colorful plastic or silk flowers from it. Once hummingbirds find the feeder, they will remember its location.

Refill the feeders as soon as they are empty to keep up a dependable food source. Clean the feeder at least once a week with a bottle brush. Discourage ants by suspending a plastic cup filled with water from the line leading to the feeder. Use special plastic "bee guards" to

Use colorful feeders to lure hummingbirds to places where you can easily observe them.

prevent large insects from clogging the feeder tube.

Feeders do not usually deter hummingbirds from migration. In northern climates, leave feeders in place until the last hummingbirds depart for the winter, then clean and store them for the season. In warm climates, it's okay to use hummingbird feeders throughout the year, especially on the West Coast and in the Southwest. There is growing evidence that many hummingbirds (and many species) winter in the southeastern states, where they feed on flowers, insects, and tree sap released by sapsuckers. Wintering hummingbirds should not be captured, held in greenhouses, or transported to tropical climates.

AMBROSIA FOR HUMMINGBIRDS

To prepare a batch of sugar-water for a hummingbird feeder, mix one part granulated white sugar to four parts water, then boil the solution for one or two minutes; don't let the brew turn to syrup. Cool the mixture before filling feeders and store the surplus in your refrigerator. Do not use honey, as it ferments easily and promotes a fungus growth that can prove harmful. Most feeders have enough red plastic parts to lure the birds, so it is not necessary to add red food coloring to the sugar-water.

As hummers, such as this Anna's, sip nectar, they pick up pollen on their crowns. The pollen is transferred to the next flower on which they feed.

ENCYCLOPEDIA
OF HUMMINGBIRD
PLANTS

On the following pages you will find descriptions of dozens of choice hummingbird-attracting plants for the Northeast and Midwest, Southeast, western mountains and deserts, and the Pacific Coast of the U.S. and Canada. Most of the selected plants are natives that occur naturally within each region, or they are common, non-invasive garden plants. Cultivars and related species are listed only if they are attractive to hummingbirds. In addition to the featured plants for every region, each section includes a list of "other good choices," some of which are recommended for adjacent regions. Note the hardiness zones for each selection, to help you choose plants that are likely to survive winter conditions in your area. A map of the USDA hardiness zones is on page 106.

HUMMINGBIRD PLANTS FOR THE NORTHEAST AND MIDWEST

STEPHEN W. KRESS

Monarda didyma

BEE BALM, BERGAMOT, OSWEGO TEA
Monarda didyma

NATIVE HABITAT Eastern North America

GROWTH TYPE Clump-forming herbaceous perennial that can spread vigorously into adjacent areas

HARDINESS ZONES 4-9

FLOWER COLOR Scarlet, pink, or lavender flowers about 1 inch long appearing in one or two whorls at the ends of stems that arise above the leaves

HEIGHT 3 feet with a spread to 2 feet

BLOOMING PERIOD Early to late summer

HOW TO GROW Full or partial sun in well-drained soils; cut back after flowering.

CULTIVARS AND RELATED SPECIES
M. fistulosa, wild bee balm, is a bushy, clump-forming perennial of eastern North American meadows with purple or pale pink flowers in late summer and early fall; 4 feet high with a spread of 18 inches; Zones 3-9.

BUTTERFLY WEED
Asclepias tuberosa

NATIVE HABITAT Prairies of central and eastern U.S.
GROWTH TYPE Herbaceous annual; typical milkweed shape
HARDINESS ZONES 4-9
FLOWER COLOR Broad clusters of bright orange flowers
HEIGHT 6 inches to 3 feet
BLOOMING PERIOD Early to late summer
HOW TO GROW Requires well-drained, sandy soils in full sun. Spring growth starts late, so do not overwater or disturb dormant plants.
NOTE: Butterflies and hummingbirds obtain nectar from the flowers; hummingbirds also take insects that are attracted to the sweet nectar.

CANNA, INDIAN SHOT
Canna species

NATIVE HABITAT Forest borders of Asia and tropical North and South America
GROWTH TYPE Herbaceous,

Asclepias tuberosa

noted for large, paddle-shaped leaves and spectacular flowers
HARDINESS ZONES Annual in Northeast
FLOWER COLOR Red, orange, pink, yellow
HEIGHT 2 to 7 feet
BLOOMING PERIOD Midsummer to early autumn
HOW TO GROW In the Northeast, plant cannas as annuals, or lift rhizomes and store, replanting in the spring after risk of frost.

CARDINAL FLOWER
Lobelia cardinalis

NATIVE HABITAT Eastern and southwestern U.S.

Heuchera sanguinea

GROWTH TYPE Perennial herb
HARDINESS ZONES 3-9
FLOWER COLOR Many scarlet flowers arise from 12- to 18-inch flower stalks; white, pink, and violet varieties also occur, but these are less attractive to hummingbirds.
HEIGHT 2 to 3 feet
BLOOMING PERIOD Early to late summer
HOW TO GROW Purchase container-grown plants or grow from seed in damp soil in full sun.
CULTIVARS AND RELATED SPECIES *L. siphilitica*, great blue lobelia, is a clump-forming perennial with erect, leafy stems with tubular, two-lipped flowers.

CINNAMON FERN
Osmunda cinnamomea

NATIVE HABITAT Most woodlands and forest edges of eastern North America
GROWTH TYPE Perennial; the cinnamon fuzz on the base of the fronds is a favorite hummingbird nest-lining material
HARDINESS ZONE 4-8
FRUITING STRUCTURE Each fertile frond is topped by a mass of cinnamon-brown sporangia in spring.
HEIGHT 36 inches tall with a spread of 24 inches
HOW TO GROW Plant in moist fertile, acidic, humus-rich soil. Grows best in partial shade or dappled light.

CORAL BELLS
Heuchera sanguinea

NATIVE HABITAT Mexico and Arizona
GROWTH TYPE Clump-forming perennial noted for its rounded leaves
HARDINESS ZONES 3-8
FLOWER COLOR Pink to red flower clusters hang like tiny bells, rising about 1 to 2 feet above the ground on wiry stems.
HEIGHT The plant is only a few inches tall, but may spread to 2 feet
BLOOMING PERIOD Spring to summer

HOW TO GROW Plant in sun or partial shade in rich soil with ample water; divide plants in early spring, removing dead growth.
CULTIVARS AND RELATED SPECIES *H.* x *brizoides* 'Firefly' features clusters of vermilion flowers, borne in short-branched panicles to 30 inches tall. *H. sanguinea* 'Firesprite' bears panicles of bright, rose-red flowers on stiff, 20-inch stems. *H. sanguinea* 'Frosty' has silver-variegated leaves and bright red flowers on 20-inch stems.

FIRE PINK
Silene virginica

NATIVE HABITAT Open woods and rocky slopes
GROWTH TYPE Herbaceous perennial
HARDINESS ZONES 4-8
FLOWER COLOR Scarlet
HEIGHT 1 to 2 feet
BLOOMING PERIOD Spring and early summer
HOW TO GROW Plant in partial shade
CULTIVARS AND RELATED SPECIES *S. regia*, royal catchfly, and *S. rotundifolia*, round-leaved catchfly, are similar to fire pink, differing in flower and leaf shape. All three species have brilliant red petals and compelling nectar supplies that lure hummingbird visitors.

FRINGED BLEEDING HEART
Dicentra eximia

NATIVE HABITAT Northeastern U.S. forests
GROWTH TYPE Perennial herb, forming non-spreading clumps
HARDINESS ZONES 4-8
FLOWER COLOR Fuchsia-red
HEIGHT 1 foot
BLOOMING PERIOD Blooms May to June; cut back in July for second blooming period in August.
HOW TO GROW Plant in rich, light, moist, porous soil; avoid letting water stand over roots; vegetation dies back in winter, so mark location of plants to avoid disturbance during the dormant period.

Dicentra eximia

CULTIVARS AND RELATED SPECIES 'Bacchanal' is a rhizomatous perennial with fine, gray-green leaves and 1-inch long crimson flowers in mid- and late spring; grows 1 foot high with a spread of 2 feet. 'Luxuriant' is a hybrid between *D. eximia* and *D. peregrina* with crimson flowers capable of thriving in full sun.

FUCHSIAS
Fuchsia species

NATIVE HABITAT Most species originated in the mountainous regions of Central and South America or New Zealand.
GROWTH TYPE Shrub or pros-

Fuchsia triphylla

trate plant suitable for hanging baskets. Nectar-production capacity of many hybrids is unknown; select varieties with simple red flowers. Typically grown as annuals in the Northeast.
HOW TO GROW Fuchsias prefer cool, low-humidity conditions; avoid windy locations. Regular misting helps. Feed with a high-nitrogen fertilizer to encourage new growth in spring; high-potassium fertilizer in summer encourages continued flowering.
CULTIVARS AND RELATED SPECIES *F. magellanica* produces small red flowers throughout the summer; in Zones 6-9, it can grow into a 10-foot tall shrub with a spread of 6 to 10 feet. In colder zones, use it and red-flowered cultivars as annual plantings. *F. triphylla* 'Mary' has many 1-inch, tube-shaped, crimson flowers born on upright woody stems.

HUMMINGBIRD'S MINT, WILD HYSSOP
Agastache cana

NATIVE HABITAT Western Texas
GROWTH TYPE Spreading perennial herb
HARDINESS ZONES 5-10
FLOWER COLOR Dark pink to orange
HEIGHT 1 to 2 feet
BLOOMING PERIOD Late summer to autumn
HOW TO GROW Full sun,

drought-tolerant; low-maintenance
CULTIVARS AND RELATED SPECIES 'Firebird' is a 2- to 6-foot perennial with coppery red-orange flowers and woody base to stems. *A. barberi*, giant hummingbird's mint, is a 2-foot tall shrubby perennial with 12-inch long spikes of rose to light magenta flowers from midsummer to fall, Zones 6-10. *A.* 'Tutti-frutti' is an erect, scented, 2- to 6-foot tall perennial with raspberry-red flowers on loose spikes from midsummer to late fall.

JEWELWEED
Impatiens capensis

NATIVE HABITAT Forest understory and edge in damp soils of eastern U.S.
GROWTH TYPE Herbaceous wildflower
HARDINESS ZONES Annual
FLOWER COLOR Orange
HEIGHT 1 to 3 feet
BLOOMING PERIOD Summer to fall
HOW TO GROW Collect seeds from wild and scatter onto bare garden soil.
CULTIVARS AND RELATED SPECIES *I. pallida*, yellow jewelweed, grows 2- to 4-feet tall and occurs in more shaded habitats than *I. capensis*. Cultivated impatiens such as *I. balsamina* and New Guinea hybrid impatiens have less nectar than *I. capensis* and *I. pallida* and are therefore

Impatiens capensis

less useful for hummingbirds, even though bright colors may prove initially attractive.

NASTURTIUM
Tropaeoleum majus

NATIVE HABITAT Cool, mountainous areas of Central and South America
GROWTH TYPE Trailing groundcover or climber
HARDINESS ZONES Annual in the Northeast
FLOWER COLOR 1- to 2-inch long, red, orange, and yellow funnel-shaped flowers have five petals.
HEIGHT 3 to 10 feet, with a spread of 5 to 15 feet

NORTHEAST & MIDWEST

BLOOMING PERIOD Summer to fall

HOW TO GROW Plant seeds in spring or nursery-grown small plants in spring or summer in full or partial sun; avoid nitrogen fertilizers to encourage flower growth.

CULTIVARS AND RELATED SPECIES Many dwarf varieties are derived from *T. majus.*

RED BUCKEYE
Aesculus pavia

NATIVE HABITAT Eastern U.S.
GROWTH TYPE Shrub or small tree
HARDINESS ZONES 5-8
FLOWER COLOR Red or sometimes marked with yellow, borne in 6-inch long, conical clusters in spring
HEIGHT 10 to 25 feet with a spread of 10 feet
BLOOMING PERIOD Late spring to early summer
HOW TO GROW Plant in full sun or partial shade in acid, alkaline, or wet soils; best to buy trees that are balled and wrapped in burlap or in containers to retain the long tap root. Prone to leaf scorch, leaf blotch, and moths; prune in early spring as necessary.

RED MORNING GLORY
Ipomoea coccinea

NATIVE HABITAT Eastern North

America
GROWTH TYPE Vine
HARDINESS ZONES Annual
FLOWER COLOR Clusters of three to eight scarlet flowers, ¾ inch in diameter, with yellow throats
HEIGHT 6 to 12 feet
BLOOMING PERIOD Summer
HOW TO GROW Soak seeds for 24 hours and plant in well-drained soil in full sun.

SCARLET RUNNER BEAN
Phaseolus coccineus

NATIVE HABITAT Widely distributed
GROWTH TYPE Climbing or bush
HARDINESS ZONES Annual
FLOWER COLOR Scarlet
HEIGHT Climbing varieties reach 8 to 12 feet; bush varieties are self-supporting and grow to only 1 to 2 feet
BLOOMING PERIOD Midsummer to early fall
HOW TO GROW Plant seeds in full sun long after risk of last frost. Support vines on a trellis or fence. Bush varieties can be grown in containers. Water frequently.

SCARLET SAGE
Salvia splendens

NATIVE HABITAT Tropical South America

Polygonatum biflorum

GROWTH TYPE Herbaceous
HARDINESS ZONES Grown as an annual in Northeast
FLOWER COLOR Scarlet red, ½- to 2-inch long, borne in slender, open terminal spikes
HEIGHT 1 to 3 feet
BLOOMING PERIOD Summer to autumn
HOW TO GROW Part sun to shade, rich soil with plenty of water.
CULTIVARS AND RELATED SPECIES *S. elegans* (*S. rutilans*), pineapple sage, is an annual herb, 2 to 3 feet tall with woolly, light green leaves, fruity taste to leaves, and red spikes in the fall. *S. coccinea* 'Lady in Red', tropical sage, is a 1-foot tall annual herb with scarlet-red flowers.

SOLOMON'S SEAL
Polygonatum biflorum

NATIVE HABITAT Forests of eastern North America
GROWTH TYPE Perennial herb
HARDINESS ZONES 3-9
FLOWER COLOR White, bell-shaped flowers that dangle from alternate leaf axils
HEIGHT 1 to 3 feet
BLOOMING PERIOD Late spring to midsummer
HOW TO GROW Plant in a cool, shady location in fertile, well-drained soil; new growth occurs as rhizomes spread to adjacent habitat. Ideal for the north side of a building or another shady location.

WILD COLUMBINE
Aquilegia canadensis

NATIVE HABITAT Forest edge from eastern Canada to Florida
GROWTH TYPE Perennial herb
HARDINESS ZONES 3-8
FLOWER COLOR Many nodding red flowers with yellow centers
HEIGHT 1 to 2 feet with a spread of 1 foot
BLOOMING PERIOD Late spring to early summer
HOW TO GROW Partial sun to full sun; prefers damp soil, but will not grow in soggy soil; protect from wind; cut back old stems for a second crop of flowers; leave seeds to feed juncos and sparrows; old plants may need to be replaced every three years.
CULTIVARS AND RELATED SPECIES Cultivated varieties with red or orange flowers are especially attractive to hummingbirds.

ZINNIA
Zinnia elegans

NATIVE HABITAT Mexico
GROWTH TYPE Herbaceous
HARDINESS ZONE Annual
FLOWER COLOR Daisy-like flower heads with many petals
HEIGHT 24 to 30 inches
HOW TO GROW Plant seeds or greenhouse-grown plants in well-drained soil in full sun after the risk of late frost; sow seeds in succession for a longer display.

CULTIVARS AND RELATED SPECIES Bright red cultivars such as 'Dreamland Scarlet' are most attractive to hummingbirds. After bloom, leave dead seed heads on zinnias and perennial composites such as purple coneflower, *Echinacea purpurea* and *E. angustifolia.* Dried seeds are readily eaten by goldfinches.

NOTE: Members of the sunflower family such as zinnias and coneflowers produce relatively little nectar, but they are highly attractive to insects, an essential component of the hummingbird diet.

Aquilegia canadensis

MORE HUMMINGBIRD PLANTS FOR THE NORTHEAST & MIDWEST

TREES
TULIP TREE *Liriodendron tulipifera*—A canopy tree with large, tulip-like green flowers with orange centers; Zones 5-9.

SHRUBS
BUTTONBUSH *Cephalanthus occidentalis*—A shrub that thrives in damp soils; flowers in spring; Zones 4-8.
FLOWERING QUINCE *Chaenomeles japonica*—A shrub with pink or orange flowers in spring; Zones 5-9.
FLY HONEYSUCKLE *Lonicera canadensis*—A 5-foot tall, native deciduous shrub with yellow, paired flowers; Zones 4-7.

VINES
CORAL HONEYSUCKLE *Lonicera sempervirens*—A climbing vine or ground cover with coral-red tubular flowers; Zones 4-9.
TRUMPET CREEPER *Campsis radicans*—Vine with orange or red tubular flowers; Zones 5-9.

PERENNIALS AND ANNUALS
DELPHINIUM (LARKSPUR) *Delphinium nudicaule*—Perennial (Zone 5-7) and *D. grandiflorum*—annual, many cultivars.
FOXGLOVE BEARDSTONGUE *Penstemon digitalis*—Perennial tolerant of high heat and humidity; Zones 2-8. *P. hirsutus* has pale violet flowers; Zones 3-9.
HOSTA (PLANTAIN LILY) *Hosta* species—Grown mainly for foliage; shade-tolerant with white or blue tubular flowers; Zones 3-8.
INDIAN PAINTBRUSH *Castilleja coccinea*—Plant from seed; full sun with bright orange flowers; Zones 5-7.
RED HOT POKER *Kniphofia uvaria*—A 4-foot tall native of South Africa; orange-yellow wands of tubular flowers; Zones 5-9.
ROSE OF SHARON *Hibiscus syriacus*—An erect, deciduous shrub with large, trumpet-shaped pink flowers; Zones 5-9.
TURTLEHEAD *Chelone glabra*—A herbaceous perennial of damp soils; Zones 4-9.

HUMMINGBIRD PLANTS FOR THE SOUTHEAST

JESSE GRANTHAM

ANISE SAGE
Salvia guaranitica

NATIVE HABITAT Widespread in South America
GROWTH TYPE Sturdy upright perennial
HARDINESS ZONES 8-9
FLOWER COLOR Deep, rich blue; flowers tubular and lipped at the ends
HEIGHT 1 to 5 feet
BLOOMING PERIOD Summer to fall
HOW TO GROW Generally well-drained garden soil in full sun to partial shade. Will need water during prolonged summer dry periods. In colder areas throughout the Southeast can be grown as an annual.
CULTIVARS AND RELATED SPECIES See other salvias.

Left: *Salvia guaranitica*
Right: *Tecomaria capensis*

CAPE HONEYSUCKLE
Tecomaria capensis

NATIVE HABITAT The only plant in this section not native to

North America, *Tecomaria* is native to South Africa
GROWTH TYPE Long-stemmed, upright shrub that can be trained to a trellis or fence; can stand on its own with frequent pruning.
HARDINESS ZONES 8-9
HOW TO GROW In sandy to rich garden soils, along fences as a foundation planting or standing alone. Established plants can withstand brief cold snaps of below-freezing temperatures. In milder climates will flower sporadically throughout the winter.

CORAL BEAN
Erythrina herbacea

NATIVE HABITAT Southwestern

U.S. south to Texas and Mexico in open fields, woodland, and oak mottes
GROWTH TYPE Upright herbaceous perennial to small, twiggy shrub
HARDINESS ZONE 9
FLOWER COLOR Dull pink to scarlet-red, long, tapered, tubular-shaped flowers
HEIGHT 2 feet
BLOOMING PERIOD Early spring; in more temperate areas flowers appear before foliage
HOW TO GROW Can grow in sand, caliche, or rich woodland soil, and is generally drought-tolerant. Prefers full sun to only light shade; fairly tolerant of light freezes where it will die back to the ground. Difficult to transplant from the wild, or to move well-established plants.
CULTIVARS AND RELATED SPECIES *E. crista-galli,* native to eastern South America, has tree-like growth habit and large red flowers. Can take short freezes. Both species visited by orioles in spring.

CORAL HONEYSUCKLE
Lonicera sempervirens

NATIVE HABITAT Edges of deciduous woodlands, field hedgerows, open woodlands as far north as lower New England states
GROWTH TYPE Non-aggressive, twining vine

Erythrina herbacea

HARDINESS ZONES 5-9; can take prolonged freezes

FLOWER COLOR Loose clusters of red to orange-red or even reddish yellow, 2-inch long, trumpet-shaped flowers with orange tips

HEIGHT Depends on support structure. Will grow well on fences, trellis, and trees to 20 feet.

BLOOMING PERIOD Throughout the growing season, with one or two periods of heavy bloom in spring or fall.

HOW TO GROW Does best in good garden soil in full sun with adequate water. Plants in shade have fewer blooms and put on more growth.

Ipomoea quamoclit

CROSS-VINE
Bignonia capreolata

NATIVE HABITAT Throughout the Southeast and as far north as Pennsylvania

GROWTH TYPE Climbing, clinging vine not unlike trumpet creeper

HARDINESS ZONES 7-9

FLOWER COLOR A broad, trumpet-shaped, red flower to 2 inches, with yellow tips. Some forms are entirely red.

HEIGHT Depends on support structure. Can cling to cement, masonry, or brick walls and grow to 20 feet.

BLOOMING PERIOD Flowers most profusely in early spring with occasional blooms throughout the summer

HOW TO GROW Can grow in full sun (best) to partial shade of open woodland. In garden situation plant in deep, rich soil on a trellis, arbor, or side of brick or stone wall for best effect.

CYPRESS VINE
Ipomoea quamoclit

NATIVE HABITAT Throughout the Southeast

GROWTH TYPE Twining vine

HARDINESS ZONES Annual

FLOWER COLOR A scarlet-red, trumpet-shaped flower to 1 inch

HEIGHT Depending on support structure, can climb to 20 feet
BLOOMING PERIOD Throughout the summer
HOW TO GROW Prefers good, rich, well-drained soil. Seedlings appear in spring under last year's plant. Purchase nursery-started plants in spring for quicker growth.

FIREBUSH
Hamelia patens

NATIVE HABITAT From southern Florida to Central and South America
GROWTH TYPE Robust, full, round-topped shrub with bright, gray-green leaves
HARDINESS ZONE 9
FLOWER COLOR Leaf stalks as well as flowers are red
HEIGHT 3 to 10 feet in good growing conditions
BLOOMING PERIOD Summer and throughout fall
HOW TO GROW A great hummingbird plant. This small shrub, grown in a landscape situation in an open yard or as a close foundation planting, does best in full sun; tolerates some light shade. Requires good moisture and well-drained soil. Summer growth is rapid and full. In the Deep South established plants can withstand brief temperatures in the 20s F., although the plant will die back to the ground.

FIRECRACKER PLANT
Russelia equisetiformis

NATIVE HABITAT Mexico and Central America
GROWTH TYPE Loose upright to weeping plant with bright green, pencil-sized stems
HARDINESS ZONE 9
FLOWER COLOR Small, bright red, tubular flowers 1 inch long
HEIGHT 1 to 3 feet tall; long stems can be tied to stakes for upright growth
BLOOMING PERIOD Throughout summer and fall in hot climates
HOW TO GROW Does well in sandy to rich loam soils. Fairly drought-tolerant. Spreads from roots, sending up shoots around base of plant. Even established plants have difficulty surviving below freezing temperatures for short periods, but the plant is readily available for replanting where killing frost occurs.

PIEDMONT RHODODENDRON
Rhododendron minus

NATIVE HABITAT Deciduous woodlands and mountains of Southeast
GROWTH TYPE Small spreading shrub
HARDINESS ZONES 6-8
FLOWER COLOR Clusters of deep red to pink flowers
HEIGHT To 3 feet
BLOOMING PERIOD Spring

Lantana camara

HOW TO GROW Will do best planted in rich soil in wooded understory on slopes. A wonderful plant for a woodland garden, but can be tricky to grow because of variations in soil pH. Mulch with pine needles or compost.

CULTIVARS AND RELATED SPECIES There are many native and non-native species of *Rhododendron*. But to attract hummingbirds and moths, use only native species.

LANTANA
Lantana camara

NATIVE HABITAT Grows from Florida to Texas and along the Gulf Coastal Plain

GROWTH TYPE Upright, stiff, twiggy perennial to low-growing shrub in the mid-South

HARDINESS ZONES 7-9

FLOWER COLOR A wide variety of colors from pink, yellow, and purple mixes to solid orange, red, and mixes in between

HEIGHT 2 to 6 feet

BLOOMING PERIOD Throughout the growing season

HOW TO GROW Prefers full sun in open situations. Somewhat tolerant of frost and short freezes; cover during extreme freezes, and some may survive. Becomes leggy and sparsely flowered in partial shade to full shade. Can grow in sandy caliche to rich loam; drought-tolerant. Birds love the fruit.

Cuphea micropetala

NOTE: Lantana flowers are mostly frequented by butterflies. Individual flowers are very small, so hummingbirds must visit many clusters to satisfy their needs.

LYRE-LEAVED SAGE
Salvia lyrata

NATIVE HABITAT Meadows of the Southeast
GROWTH TYPE Single stalk arising from a rosette of basal leaves
HARDINESS ZONES 7-8
FLOWER COLOR Pale blue to white
HEIGHT 1 to 2 feet
BLOOMING PERIOD For a month in early spring
HOW TO GROW Naturalizes in open lawns and meadows. Start from seed, then mow lawns or meadows after flowering is over. This encourages dense stands.
CULTIVARS AND RELATED SPECIES See other salvias.

MEXICAN CIGAR
Cuphea micropetala

NATIVE HABITAT From Mexico to Central America
GROWTH TYPE Small mounded shrub to about 3 feet
HARDINESS ZONES 8-9; not terribly frost-tolerant, but can be grown as an annual in more temperate areas
FLOWER COLOR Bright red, tubular-shaped flowers with yellow tips, about 1 inch long
HEIGHT 1 to 3 feet
BLOOMING PERIOD Summer through fall
HOW TO GROW Grows well along borders or as a foundation plant in full sun to partial light shade.
CULTIVARS AND RELATED SPECIES *C. hyssopifolia,* an evergreen sub-shrub from Mexico and Guatemala, is also popular.

MEXICAN BUSH SAGE
Salvia leucantha

NATIVE HABITAT Higher elevations in Central and Eastern Mexico
GROWTH TYPE Multi-stemmed perennial throughout its cultivat-

ed range in the U.S.
HARDINESS ZONES 7-9
FLOWER COLOR Curved, tubular flowers are white and emerge from a purple calyx.
HEIGHT Can grow up to 4 feet in a season and 3 to 5 feet in diameter.
BLOOMING PERIOD Generally from late summer to frost
HOW TO GROW Can grow in sandy to rich, well-drained soil and does best in full sun; drought-tolerant. Prune dead stalks to ground after frost. Can withstand freezing temperatures for short periods, but tops will die back to the ground. In cooler areas of the Southeast, works best as a foundation planting.
CULTIVARS AND RELATED SPECIES See other salvias.

Salvia leucantha

MEXICAN HONEYSUCKLE
Justicia spicigera

NATIVE HABITAT Dry areas of the Southwest and Mexico
GROWTH TYPE Spreads by underground stems, forming a multi-stemmed, compact clump
HARDINESS ZONE 9
BLOOMING PERIOD In areas of the Deep South (coastal Texas, southern Florida) plants bloom all year, but seem to bloom most profusely in fall and winter.
HOW TO GROW Because of winter flowering periods, this is a great plant for overwintering hummingbirds. Grows best in full sun and in cooler areas, and is most successful as a foundation plant on south-facing walls. Transplant from clumps. Established plants in the Deep

SOUTHEAST

South can withstand brief temperatures below freezing. Tops will die back and plant will resprout from base in spring.
CULTIVARS AND RELATED SPECIES All justicias are excellent hummingbird plants.

MOUNTAIN SAGE
Salvia regla

NATIVE HABITAT From the Chisos Mountains of Texas south to Mexico
GROWTH TYPE In warmer climates it can be a rather robust, many-stemmed, small shrub.
HARDINESS ZONES 8-9; can withstand temperatures down to 20 degrees F.
FLOWER COLOR Deep rose-red

HEIGHT In protected and warm locations can reach 6 feet, 4 to 5 feet wide.
BLOOMING PERIOD Like many salvias, this is a fall-blooming plant. Will bloom until there is a frost or days grow short.
HOW TO GROW In cooler climates does best on east- or south-facing walls with light shade. In warmer climates does well in any garden setting with partial shade. Prefers good soil and drainage.
CULTIVARS AND RELATED SPECIES See other salvias.

SHRIMP PLANT
Justicia brandegeana

NATIVE HABITAT Native to Mexico, but has naturalized in some places on the Texas Coastal Plain
GROWTH TYPE Herbaceous; sprawling to leggy plant, will grow up among branches of shrubs and small trees.
HARDINESS ZONES 8-9 Established plants can survive light frost in more temperate climates.
FLOWER COLOR White tubular flowers speckled with pink emerge from pink to red bracts.
HEIGHT 1 to 4 or 5 feet when growing among shrubs
BLOOMING PERIOD Spring to fall
HOW TO GROW Full sun to light

Justicia brandegeana

shade; does well as container plant and can be kept indoors in winter. Survives frost when planted as a foundation plant on south-facing wall in more temperate climates.

CULTIVARS AND RELATED SPECIES There are many species of *Justicia*, all favored by hummingbirds.

SLEEPY MALLOW, SULTAN'S TURBAN
Malvaviscus arboreus var. *drummondii*

NATIVE HABITAT Found naturally in open sunny glades, roadsides, or forest oak motte understory with partial sun. Common along Gulf Coastal Plain.

GROWTH TYPE Rather upright, leggy perennial in partial shade; sturdy upright perennial in full sun

HARDINESS ZONES 7-9 Deciduous in colder zones from Florida to Texas. Hardy north to Tennessee/Mississippi border.

FLOWER COLOR Bright scarlet-red, upright, closed flowers at the top of branches or leaf clusters

HEIGHT 1 to 8 feet

BLOOMING PERIOD Throughout the growing season and until the onset of cool weather

HOW TO GROW Grows in many different soil types from sand/caliche to rich, deep loamy soils. Can tolerate drought conditions. Does well in perennial borders and foundation plantings in full sun to partial shade.

CULTIVARS AND RELATED SPECIES *M. arboreus* var. *mexicanus* also occurs in North America. It has larger, more open flowers, and is not as hardy as var. *drummondii*.

TEXAS OLIVE
Cordia boissieri

NATIVE HABITAT Coastal areas to dry semi-desert regions of Texas and Mexico

GROWTH TYPE An evergreen, this medium-sized tree is evenly proportioned, with a rounded form.

HARDINESS ZONE Zone 9 only; sensitive to below-freezing temperatures for any length of time. Frost will kill leaves, but plant will leaf out in spring.

FLOWER COLOR Abundant, beautiful white azalea-like flowers with yellow throats. Flowers are favored by hummingbirds during spring migration.

HEIGHT Tall specimens may reach 8 to 10 feet.

BLOOMING PERIOD During spring months and sometimes again in fall

HOW TO GROW This tree grows in full sun or open shade in hot humid or dry regions. Can be grown in many different soil types from rich sandy loam to sand/caliche; very drought-tolerant; requires water first year after planting.

SOUTHEAST

TROPICAL SAGE
Salvia coccinea

NATIVE HABITAT Found throughout the tropics; in recent years has spread to tropical North America
GROWTH TYPE Rather loose, upright annual to perennial in milder climates
HARDINESS ZONE 9
FLOWER COLOR Many varieties from deep red to white
HEIGHT To 3 feet

BLOOMING PERIOD Throughout the growing season
HOW TO GROW In milder regions of the Southeast, this plant can be a perennial. Cooler temperatures will reduce it to a basal rosette in winter. Heavy frost or a freeze will kill the plant, but seeds survive the winter and germinate in spring. Start with 6- to 8-inch nursery-started plants in spring in loamy garden soil. Seedlings will appear where last

MORE HUMMINGBIRD PLANTS FOR THE SOUTHEAST

TREES
RED BUCKEYE *Aesculus pavia*—An understory large shrub to small tree of deep deciduous forests. Produces racemes of bright red, tubular flowers in early spring before other forest trees are in full leaf. Produces a striking effect; Zones 5-8.

SHRUBS
FIRE SPIKE *Odontonema strictum*—A tropical evergreen, which grows in full sun to partial shade. Crimson-red flowers are borne on terminal spikes in late fall. Flowers until hard frost; Zones 8-9.
SWAMP AZALEA *Rhododendron viscosum*—A medium-sized shrub of moist woodland edges. Pale red flowers with white edging appear in early spring; Zones 7-8.

VINES
MEXICAN FLAME VINE *Pseudogynoxys chenopodioides*—An 8- to 10-foot vine with big clusters of 1-inch, orange-red flowers. Plants will bloom throughout the year where winters are mild; Zone 9 only.

PERENNIALS AND ANNUALS
AUTUMN SAGE *Salvia greggii*—This plant of the dry West does surprisingly well in humid coastal areas and in more temperate climates. Does best in full sun and is drought-tolerant; Zones 7-9.

year's plants bloomed. Requires occasional watering during dry periods in summer.
CULTIVARS AND RELATED SPECIES See other salvias.

TRUMPET CREEPER
Campsis radicans

NATIVE HABITAT Throughout the southeastern U.S. to southern New England
GROWTH TYPE Climbing, clinging vine. Can grow up smooth surfaces via attachment by aerial roots.
HARDINESS ZONES 5-8
FLOWER COLOR Orange to orange-yellow flowers 2 to 4 inches long
HEIGHT Depends on support structure. Can climb to the top of telephone poles, tall trees, or buildings.
BLOOMING PERIOD Sporadically in spring; heavily in late summer through fall
HOW TO GROW In deep, rich topsoil in full sun on fences, trellis, or arbors. Prune throughout the summer to keep in check.

SOUTHEAST

CARDINAL FLOWER *Lobelia cardinalis*—One of the most spectacular hummingbird plants for the eastern half of the U.S. Prefers partial shade to full sun and rich garden soil and moisture. A strong, erect plant with spikes covered with bright red, lipped flowers; Zones 3-9.
CORAL BELLS *Heuchera americana*—Grown in the nursery trade mainly for its foliage, but has tall, 3-foot spikes covered with small greenish white flowers in early spring; Zones 4-8.
DESERT HONEYSUCKLE *Anisacanthus wrightii*—This dense, spreading plant has deep orange-red, trumpet-shaped flowers. Does better in the coastal South where winter temperatures are milder; cannot take hard freezes; Zones 8-9.
MEXICAN MILKWEED *Asclepias curassavica*—A tall, tropical milkweed with yellow-orange flowers. Goes well with lantana, tropical sage, and sultan's cap; Zones 7-9.
VIRGINIA BLUEBELLS *Mertensia virginica*—A native to the eastern U.S. usually found along streams or in alluvial plains. Loose clusters of drooping blue flowers on 1- to 2-foot stems. Flowers appear early in spring. Foliage dies back in summer; Zones 3-7.
WILD COLUMBINE *Aquilegia canadensis*—A small woodland perennial 1- to 2-feet tall. A native to eastern and central North America with red and yellow drooping flowers 1 inch long. Prefers cooler woodland areas of Zones 7-8.

Castilleja chromosa, desert paintbrush

HUMMINGBIRD PLANTS FOR THE WESTERN MOUNTAINS AND DESERTS

LYNN HASSLER KAUFMAN

ARIZONA THISTLE
Cirsium arizonicum

NATIVE HABITAT Rocky slopes and roadsides, 3,000 to 7,000 feet in Utah and Arizona
GROWTH TYPE Biennial
HARDINESS ZONES 6-8
FLOWER COLOR Red
HEIGHT 2 feet
BLOOMING PERIOD May to October
HOW TO GROW Although thistles are considered weeds in many parts of the country, this species does not seem to reseed readily. Grow in full sun in well-drained soil. Plant away from walkways since the foliage is spiny and prickly. May be diffi-cult to find, but seeds are available.
CULTIVARS AND RELATED SPECIES New Mexico thistle (*C. neomexicanum*) grows from 1,000 to 6,500 feet in the Southwest; has lavender blooms, March to September.

BAJA FAIRY DUSTER
Calliandra californica

NATIVE HABITAT Gravelly flats, hillsides, and washes in the central desert of Baja California, Mexico
GROWTH TYPE This shrub has flowers like fluffy balls or brushes. It's rich in nectar and insect

Calliandra eriophylla, fairy duster

life and is extremely popular with hummingbirds.

HARDINESS ZONES 9-10
FLOWER COLOR Spectacular bright red "powder puff" blooms
HEIGHT 4 to 5 feet
BLOOMING PERIOD Nearly year-round in warmer desert areas
HOW TO GROW Plant in full sun for optimal blooming; tolerates light shade. Not picky about soil type. Natural growth form is attractive and needs no shaping.
CULTIVARS AND RELATED SPECIES Fairy duster (*Calliandra eriophylla*) is native to southwestern U.S. and Mexico. Generally found at 1,000 to 5,000 feet in sandy washes, dry gravelly slopes, and mesas. Flowers (primarily February to May) range from nearly white to deep pink. Hardy to 10 degrees F.; drought-tolerant. Foliage is evergreen to semi-evergreen, depending on temperatures and availability of moisture.

CHUPAROSA
Justicia californica

NATIVE HABITAT Desert areas of southern Arizona, southeastern California into Mexico; rocky slopes and along washes 1,000 to 4,000 feet
GROWTH TYPE Shrub; chuparosa means "hummingbird" in Spanish. The slender floral tubes contain abundant nectar.
HARDINESS ZONES 8-10

FLOWER COLOR Bright red; a yellow-flowering variety is available in the landscape trade.
HEIGHT 3 feet tall and 4 feet wide; can reach 6 feet under ideal conditions
BLOOMING PERIOD Heaviest in spring, but also summer, fall, and winter if not frozen back
HOW TO GROW Plant in full sun. Very drought-tolerant once established. Can be grown on 10 inches or less of annual rainfall, but periodic watering will improve appearance.
CULTIVARS AND RELATED SPECIES Red justicia (*J. candicans*) sports lush green leaves and bright red-orange flowers February to May. Native to canyons and washes, 1,500 to 3,500 feet, in southern Arizona and northern Mexico. Reaches 3 feet. Fast-growing and likes supplemental water.

CORAL BELLS
Heuchera versicolor

NATIVE HABITAT Moist, shaded rocks in coniferous forests, 6,500 to 12,000 feet in southwestern U.S. and northern Mexico
GROWTH TYPE Herbaceous perennial; dainty flower stalks arise from clumps of evergreen leaves.
HARDINESS ZONES 5-8
FLOWER COLOR Mainly pink
HEIGHT 6- to 10-inch stalks
BLOOMING PERIOD May to October
HOW TO GROW Plant in shade or partial shade and provide ample water. Clumps may need to be divided after several years.
CULTIVARS AND RELATED SPECIES *H. sanguinea,* with red flowers, is native to southeastern Arizona and Mexico at elevations of 4,000 to 8,500 feet. There are many varieties of coral bells in the nursery trade.

INDIAN PAINTBRUSH
Castilleja integra

NATIVE HABITAT Dryish rocky slopes among oaks and pines in Colorado, western Texas, New Mexico, Arizona, and northern Mexico, 4,500 to 10,000 feet
GROWTH TYPE Herbaceous perennial; there are more than 200 species of paintbrush in the West, and they are important hummingbird plants.
HARDINESS ZONES 5-8
FLOWER COLOR The true flowers are inconspicuous and usually green; the large splashes of color (in this species, vermilion) are the brightly colored leafy bracts.
HEIGHT To 1 foot
BLOOMING PERIOD March to September
HOW TO GROW Most paintbrushes are partial root parasites, and seeds need to be planted with seeds of another plant (such as blue grama grass, for

WESTERN MOUNTAINS & DESERTS

this species). Long-lived when grown with a suitable host. Likes well-drained soil.

CULTIVARS AND RELATED SPECIES Desert paintbrush (*Castilleja chromosa*) is native to open sagebrush flats, 5,000 to 8,000 feet from eastern Oregon to Wyoming and south to New Mexico and southern California. Bracts are orange.

INDIAN PINK, MEXICAN CAMPION
Silene laciniata

NATIVE HABITAT Western Texas to California and Mexico, 5,500

Penstemon parryi

to 9,000 feet, mostly in pine forests

GROWTH TYPE Perennial herb; at first glance the flower petals seem separate rather than fused into tubes. A closer look reveals that the lower part of each petal is confined within a tubular calyx, thus displaying the tubular shape that is so attractive to hummingbirds.

HARDINESS ZONES 5-7

FLOWER COLOR Red

HEIGHT To 3 feet

BLOOMING PERIOD July to October

HOW TO GROW Partial shade; likes to lean against other vegetation. May be difficult to find; try native-plant nurseries or catalogs.

OCOTILLO
Fouquieria splendens

NATIVE HABITAT Arizona, California, and Texas deserts; rocky hillsides below 5,000 feet

GROWTH TYPE Thorny shrub with long, unbranched stems and flame-colored spring blooms—a distinctive accent plant. The stems are popular perches for hummingbirds.

HARDINESS ZONES 7-8

FLOWER COLOR Dense clusters of bright red, tubular blossoms appear at branch tips.

HEIGHT To 15 feet

BLOOMING PERIOD April to June, but may bloom at other seasons

HOW TO GROW Plant in full sun in well-drained soil. Susceptible to overwatering. Drops leaves when conditions are dry and leafs out in response to moisture, up to several times a year. If pruning is necessary, cut branches away at the base. Individual cane-like stems root readily and make "living fences" that develop roots, leaves, and sometimes flowers.

PARRY PENSTEMON
Penstemon parryi

NATIVE HABITAT Washes, desert slopes, and canyons of southern Arizona and Sonora, Mexico, 1,500 to 5,000 feet
GROWTH TYPE Herbaceous perennial; penstemon make up a very large genus of plants, and there are species available for nearly every climate.
HARDINESS ZONES 8-10
FLOWER COLOR Deep pink, tubular flowers
HEIGHT 2- to 3-foot flower spikes arise from basal rosette of foliage
BLOOMING PERIOD February to April
HOW TO GROW Well-drained soil, full sun. Do not overwater. Spent flower spikes can be cut off after they have gone to seed. Reseeds freely.
CULTIVARS AND RELATED SPECIES Rock penstemon (*P. baccharifolius*) grows in limestone areas in west Texas from 1,100 to 4,400 feet. Cherry-red flowers on short spikes bloom throughout the hot season in the low desert (June to September). Part shade to full sun. Prune off old flower stalks to improve the plant's appearance.

RED SAGE, AUTUMN SAGE
Salvia greggii

NATIVE HABITAT Rocky canyons from 2,200 to 5,800 feet in the Chihuahuan Desert region
GROWTH TYPE Evergreen, small, rounded shrub; this is one of the "star" introductions to the nurs-

Salvia greggii

Top: *Hesperaloe parviflora*
Bottom: *Stachys coccinea*

ery trade. It may bloom lightly throughout the year in warmer areas, providing a reliable nectar source for hummingbirds.

HARDINESS ZONES 7-10

FLOWER COLOR Spikes of tubular flowers in shades of rose-pink; many color variants are available, but those with reddish hues are particularly attractive to hummers.

HEIGHT 3 feet

BLOOMING PERIOD March to November

HOW TO GROW Part shade to full sun. Needs good drainage. Prune back hard to keep plants less woody.

CULTIVARS AND RELATED SPECIES Mountain sage or cardinal sage (*S. regla*) is a fall-bloomer in western Texas. Grows 3 to 5 feet tall (sometimes to 8 feet) and produces masses of brilliant vermilion flowers. Cedar sage (*S. roemeriana*) is a low-growing perennial about 12 inches across. Native to western Texas and Mexico. Scarlet flowers March to August. Prefers dappled shade.

RED YUCCA
Hesperaloe parviflora

NATIVE HABITAT Prairies, rocky slopes, mesquite groves in central and southwestern Texas and northern Mexico

GROWTH TYPE Evergreen perennial; this member of the agave family has an attractive form and texture and makes a nice accent plant.

HARDINESS ZONES 7-10
FLOWER COLOR Coral or salmon bell-shaped flowers in clusters; a yellow-flowering variety is now available
HEIGHT Flower stalks reach 5 feet
BLOOMING PERIOD Spring to fall
HOW TO GROW Full sun or partial shade in well-drained soil. Drought-tolerant. Prune back flower stalks after blooming.

SCARLET OR TEXAS BETONY
Stachys coccinea

NATIVE HABITAT Canyons and slopes of west Texas to southern Arizona and Mexico, 1,500 to 8,000 feet
GROWTH TYPE Herbaceous perennial; this member of the mint family forms small mounds of leaves and has a long blooming period.
HARDINESS ZONES 7-9
FLOWER COLOR Vermilion flowers whorled on dense spikes
HEIGHT 18 inches, spreading to 24 inches wide
BLOOMING PERIOD Spring through fall
HOW TO GROW Likes rich soil; requires additional water or light to medium shade to survive summer heat in high desert.

Penstemon barbatus

SCARLET BUGLER
Penstemon barbatus

NATIVE HABITAT Mountains in coniferous or oak woodlands, southern Colorado and Utah to Mexico; 4,000 to 10,000 feet
GROWTH TYPE Herbaceous perennial
HARDINESS ZONES 5-8
FLOWER COLOR Tubular red flowers in loose spikes; the lower lip of the flower in this species is bent back so hummingbirds can hover to sip the nectar. Bees and butterflies must perch to feed and have no foothold.
HEIGHT 1 to 3 feet
BLOOMING PERIOD June to October

WESTERN MOUNTAINS & DESERTS

Bouvardia glaberrima, smooth bouvardia

HOW TO GROW Well-drained soil, sun to partial shade. May be short-lived in warm winter areas.

CULTIVARS AND RELATED SPECIES Firecracker penstemon (*P. eatonii*) grows on rocky slopes of the Southwest, 2,000 to 7,000 feet. Well-drained soil in full sun to partial shade. Tubular scarlet flowers bloom March to June. Pineleaf penstemon (*P. pinnifolius*) grows on outcroppings and steep slopes from 6,000 to 8,500 feet from southern Arizona and New Mexico into Mexico. Small scarlet flowers on 10- to 12-inch spikes. Popular with White-eared Hummingbirds in Mexico.

SCARLET GILIA, SKYROCKET
Ipomopsis aggregata

NATIVE HABITAT Montana to British Columbia, south to New Mexico, Arizona, and California; 5,000 to 8,500 feet, mostly in open coniferous forests
GROWTH TYPE Biennial
HARDINESS ZONES 5-8
FLOWER COLOR Normally bright red but also pink or white; in some areas this showy wildflower changes color in response to changes in pollinators. Early in the season, red flowers are most common, coinciding with the abundance of hummingbirds in mountainous regions. By late August, new

flowering plants produce mainly light pink and white flowers, as most hummingbirds depart and sphinx moths take over as the main pollinators.

HEIGHT 2 feet
BLOOMING PERIOD May to September
HOW TO GROW Likes well-drained soil and full sun; individual plants are on the thin side, so the plant looks best in mass plantings.

SMOOTH BOUVARDIA
Bouvardia glaberrima

NATIVE HABITAT Dry shady slopes and canyons of southern New Mexico and Arizona, 3,000 to 9,000 feet
GROWTH TYPE Bouvardia belongs to a largely tropical family. This handsome shrub with neat foliage has narrow, trumpet-like flowers that flare into four lobes.
HARDINESS ZONES 6-8
FLOWER COLOR Clusters of bright red-orange (sometimes pink or white) honeysuckle-type flowers
HEIGHT 2 to 3 feet
BLOOMING PERIOD May to October
HOW TO GROW Prefers partial shade and supplemental water. Sometimes difficult to find in the landscape trade; check native-plant nurseries.

SOUTHWEST CORAL BEAN
Erythrina flabelliformis

NATIVE HABITAT Rocky canyons and hillsides in southeastern Arizona, southwestern New Mexico, and north Mexico, including Baja; 3,000 to 5,500 feet
GROWTH TYPE Shrub; when in flower or fruit, this plant is striking. At other times it has leafless brown stems.
HARDINESS ZONES 8-10
FLOWER COLOR Clusters of bright red, tubular flowers
HEIGHT 3 to 6 feet; can reach tree size in warmer areas of Mexico
BLOOMING PERIOD Spring; sometimes again after summer rains
HOW TO GROW Plant in warm location in well-drained soil. Full sun. Prune frost-damaged wood after new foliage appears. The bright red seeds are poisonous.

SUPERB PENSTEMON
Penstemon superbus

NATIVE HABITAT Rocky canyons and along washes in New Mexico, southeastern Arizona, and Chihuahua, 3,500 to 5,500 feet
GROWTH TYPE Herbaceous perennial
HARDINESS ZONES 7-10
FLOWER COLOR Dark coral

WESTERN MOUNTAINS & DESERTS

HEIGHT Flower stalks reach 3 to 4 feet

BLOOMING PERIOD April to May

HOW TO GROW In full sun; likes sandy or gravelly soils

CULTIVARS AND RELATED SPECIES See *P. barbatus* and *P. parryi*.

TREE TOBACCO
Nicotiana glauca

NATIVE HABITAT Southern Bolivia to northern Argentina, but has naturalized extensively in many parts of the West and Southeast

GROWTH TYPE This shrubby tree is a rather weedy-looking plant often seen growing by roadsides. The abundant flowers are very popular with hummingbirds.

HARDINESS ZONES 7-10

FLOWER COLOR Yellow-green tubular flowers

HEIGHT Up to 20 feet

BLOOMING PERIOD Sporadically throughout the year in warm climates

HOW TO GROW Full sun, partial shade. Fast-growing. Short lived but reseeds readily.

WESTERN LARKSPUR
Delphinium occidentale

NATIVE HABITAT Moist mountain meadows in the Rocky

Nicotiana glauca, **tree tobacco**

Tecoma stans, yellow bells

Mountains and northern Southwest
GROWTH TYPE Herbaceous perennial
HARDINESS ZONES 4-5
FLOWER COLOR Tall spires of blue-purple blooms
HEIGHT 3 to 6 feet
BLOOMING PERIOD June to August
HOW TO GROW Full sun or part shade. Seeds are available from native plant catalogs.

WOLFBERRY
Lycium andersonii

NATIVE HABITAT Desert washes and rocky slopes to 6,000 feet in southern Utah and Nevada,

Arizona, southwestern New Mexico, and northwestern Mexico
GROWTH TYPE Shrub; in addition to the short tubular flowers that attract hummingbirds, this dense, spiny shrub also produces berries that are relished by many other kinds of birds.
HARDINESS ZONES 7-10
FLOWER COLOR Pale lavender, short but tubular
HEIGHT 6 feet
BLOOMING PERIOD February to May
HOW TO GROW Plants of many species of *Lycium* are now available in one-gallon containers. Plant in full sun or light shade in well-drained soil. Best left unpruned. Becomes leafless in response to drought and cold.

CULTIVARS AND RELATED SPECIES
There are many species of wolf-berry including *L. berlandieri, L. exsertum*, and *L. fremontii*. All look rather similar and have the same white to purplish flowers that are visited by hummingbirds.

YELLOW BELLS
Tecoma stans var. *angustata*

NATIVE HABITAT 2,000 to 5,000 feet on rocky slopes, gravelly plains, and arroyos, southeastern Arizona, southern New Mexico,

MORE HUMMINGBIRD PLANTS FOR THE WESTERN MOUNTAINS AND DESERTS

TREES
DESERT WILLOW *Chilopsis linearis*—A tree of dry washes with pink to lavender trumpet-shaped flowers in clusters, April-September; Zones 7-10.

SHRUBS
CAPE HONEYSUCKLE *Tecomaria capensis*—A South African native grown as a shrub or vine; showy orange flowers in fall and winter; Zones 9-10.
GALVEZIA *Galvezia juncea*—This Baja California native bears scarlet tubular flowers on and off all year; to 6 feet; Zones 9-10.

VINES
SCARLET CREEPER *Ipomoea coccinea*—A long twining vine with reddish orange tubular flowers May to October; Zones 7-10.

PERENNIALS AND ANNUALS
CALIFORNIA FUCHSIA/HUMMINGBIRD TRUMPET *Epilobium canum* subspecies *latifolia* (formerly *Zauschneria californica* subspecies *latifolia)*—A perennial with bright red-orange, trumpet-shaped flowers late summer and fall; Zones 7-10.
CARDINAL FLOWER *Lobelia cardinalis*—A perennial with bright red, inch-long flowers June to October. Likes moist soil; Zones 5-8.
CORAL FOUNTAIN *Russelia equisetiformis*—A shrubby perennial native to Mexico with bright red, tubular flowers spring to fall; likes moist soil; Zones 9-10.
CRIMSON MONKEYFLOWER *Mimulus cardinalis*—A perennial

west Texas, south into Mexico, Central and South America
GROWTH TYPE Deciduous shrub; the lush foliage and showy blooms of this plant give it a tropical look
HARDINESS ZONES 7-9
FLOWER COLOR Yellow trumpet-shaped flowers in large clusters
HEIGHT To 5 feet
BLOOMING PERIOD April to November
HOW TO GROW Full sun and well-drained soil. Recovers quickly after frost and can grow 4 feet in a season.

with funnel-shaped red flowers March to October; likes moisture and shade; Zones 6-9.
GIANT HYSSOP *Agastache cana*—2- to 3-foot tall, rose-pink flower spikes bloom midsummer to fall; aromatic leaves; Zones 6-7.
TROPICAL SAGE, RED SAGE *Salvia coccinea*—This plant bears red flowers in spring and summer; reseeds readily; Zones 8-10.

Chilopsis linearis, desert willow

WESTERN MOUNTAINS & DESERTS

Epilobium canum subspecies *latifolia*, California fuchsia

HUMMINGBIRD PLANTS FOR THE PACIFIC COAST

BETH HUNING

CALIFORNIA FUCHSIA, HUMMINGBIRD FUCHSIA

Epilobium canum subspecies *latifolia* (formerly *Zauschneria californica* subspecies *latifolia*)

NATIVE HABITAT Dry slopes and ridges of California foothills
GROWTH TYPE Herbaceous
HARDINESS ZONES 8-10
FLOWER COLOR Bright red or red-orange, long, tubular flowers 1- to 1½-inches long with projecting stamens growing at ends of upright or arching stems. Hummers can't resist this one! If you have to choose just one plant, this should be it.
HEIGHT 4 to 20 inches
BLOOMING PERIOD Summer and fall
HOW TO GROW Drought-tolerant ground cover; thrives in hot, dry summers. Will spread throughout garden by roots and by reseeding itself. Groom in winter or it will become twiggy.

CALIFORNIA INDIAN PINK

Silene californica

NATIVE HABITAT California and southern Oregon foothills
GROWTH TYPE Herbaceous perennial sometimes treated as annual
HARDINESS ZONES 8-10
FLOWER COLOR Flowers are vermilion, 1¼-inch wide, and fringed.
HEIGHT 6 to 16 inches
BLOOMING PERIOD Spring
HOW TO GROW Can be grown from seed. Prefers filtered

Salvia clevelandii, Cleveland sage

shade; requires well-drained soil that is allowed to dry in summer. Can be grown in hanging baskets.

CLEVELAND SAGE
Salvia clevelandii

NATIVE HABITAT Chaparral and coastal sage scrub habitats of San Diego County, California
GROWTH TYPE Evergreen shrub
HARDINESS ZONES 9-10
FLOWER COLOR Clusters of blue, ¾-inch, fragrant flowers
HEIGHT To 4 feet
BLOOMING PERIOD Spring through summer
HOW TO GROW Full sun in well-drained soil. Drought-tolerant; needs very little water in summer
CULTIVARS AND RELATED SPECIES Many species of sage attract hummingbirds and thrive in the arid West. Two good ones are *S. leucantha*, Mexican bush sage; *S.* 'Allen Chickering'.

DESERT WILLOW
Chilopsis linearis

NATIVE HABITAT Open areas and stream courses of deserts and the basin and ranges of the southwestern U.S.
GROWTH TYPE Shrub, sometimes becoming tree-like
HARDINESS ZONES 7-9
FLOWER COLOR Trumpet-

shaped flowers generally purplish to pink, sometimes orange to yellow

HEIGHT Up to 20 feet; full spreading, often as broad as it is high

BLOOMING PERIOD Late spring through late summer, depending upon elevation and exposure to sun.

HOW TO GROW Thrives in direct sun in dry, open areas; is drought-tolerant and hence deciduous from late summer through mid-winter.

CULTIVARS AND RELATED SPECIES Also known as desert catalpa, *Chilopsis* is not a true willow (*Salix* species), but its elliptical leaves resemble those of willows, hence the common name "desert willow." However, *Chilopsis* should not be used interchangeably with true willows, which do not produce similar flowers. *C. linearis* 'Burgundy' has deep red-purple flowers.

Penstemon 'Sour Grapes'

FIREBIRD PENSTEMON
Penstemon gloxinioides

NATIVE HABITAT Also known as *P. hartwegii* and a hybrid with *P. cobaea;* most penstemons are native to the western U.S. and Mexico and thrive in varied habitats

GROWTH TYPE Herbaceous shrubby perennial

HARDINESS ZONES 8-10

FLOWER COLOR Deep crimson, 1-inch tubular flowers with upper lip deeply lobed; flowers clustered along but mostly near the ends of many erect stems

HEIGHT 2 to 2½ feet

BLOOMING PERIOD Spring and summer into fall if pruned after each bloom

HOW TO GROW Full sun or partial shade and well-drained sandy or loamy soils; thrives with periodic watering but subject to root rot in persistently damp soils.

CULTIVARS AND RELATED SPECIES Several named cultivars are readily available in nurseries. 'Apple Blossom' or 'Huntington Pink' has pink flowers and grows to 3 feet; 'Lady Hindley' has lavender flowers, 'Garnet' dark red, and 'Sour Grapes' purple. Many species of penstemons are important plants for humming-birds. All have tubular flowers that range in color from red, pink, and purple to true blue. Some other popular species include: *P. cardinalis*, beardstongue or scarlet bugler, which is similar to firebird penstemon, but with flowers more red than deep crimson; *P. campanulatus*, *P. labrosus*, golden beardstongue, *P. clevelandii*, *P. barbatus* 'Prairie Fire', 'Elfin Pink', and Utah hybrids.

FLOWERING CURRANT
Ribes sanguineum

NATIVE HABITAT Foothills and forested mountain slopes of western mountains to about 6,000 feet, generally in moist or damp areas
GROWTH TYPE Deciduous shrub
HARDINESS ZONES 6-8
FLOWER COLOR Hanging clusters of red tubular flowers
HEIGHT Grows to about 6 feet and can spread as wide as it grows high
BLOOMING PERIOD Spring
HOW TO GROW Hardy and easily adaptable to a variety of settings; often used as an ornamental in formal gardens. Prefers well-drained soil and full sun but will grow in semi-shade for part of the day. Slender stems can be pruned into a dense hedge.
CULTIVARS AND RELATED SPECIES There are many species of native currants and gooseberries, all with red or red and white flowers. Alternate species include: *R. malvaceum*, pink flowering currant or chaparral currant, has hanging clusters of bright pink and white flowers that bloom in early spring; requires no water once established. *R. speciosum*, fuchsia-flowered gooseberry, is an evergreen shrub with drooping, deep crimson to cherry-red flowers resembling common varieties of fuchsia; blooms winter and spring; prefers sun to light shade; tolerates drought but will lose leaves in summer if not watered.

Ribes sanguineum

INDIAN PAINTBRUSH
Castilleja coccinea

NATIVE HABITAT Dry slopes of the western U.S.
GROWTH TYPE Herbaceous
HARDINESS ZONES 6-9
FLOWER COLOR Scarlet, clustered spikes of minutely lobed ¼-inch flowers with one or two pairs of narrow lobes on upper bracts
HEIGHT 6 to 12 inches
BLOOMING PERIOD Spring to mid fall
HOW TO GROW Must be grown from seed near other plants as it parasitizes roots of other plants.
CULTIVARS AND RELATED SPECIES *Castilleja* are important hummingbird plants in the western United States. Species range in habitat and distribution from low elevation dry slopes to high mountains. The many species of paintbrush include *C. applegatei* subspecies *pinetorum* with scarlet, sometimes orange or yellow, bracts. Although Paintbrushes are not widely found in nurseries, seed is available from native plant nurseries.

IOCROMA
Iocroma cyameum

NATIVE HABITAT Tropical Central and South America
GROWTH TYPE Herbaceous perennial
HARDINESS ZONES 6-10
FLOWER COLOR Light blue, tubular, trumpet-like flowers up to 2½ inches in length, clustered at terminal ends of branches
HEIGHT Stalks to 6 feet
BLOOMING PERIOD Fall
HOW TO GROW Sun or partial sun or shade in well-drained soil; sensitive to frost; dies back in winter so best if covered but new growth will rise from hardy roots; will grow from rooted cuttings.
CULTIVARS AND RELATED SPECIES The foliage and shape of *Iocroma* resembles several species of fuchsia in appearance. Many fuchsias, such as 'Gardenmeister Bonstedt', have branches terminating in large clusters of long, red, trumpet-like flowers 2

Iocroma cyameum

Justicia spicigera

inches long. *F.* 'China House' has individual flowers in multiple shades of pink protruding from down-swept branches.

ISLAND BUSH SNAPDRAGON
Galvezia speciosa

NATIVE HABITAT Santa Catalina, San Clemente, and Guadalupe Islands off the Pacific Coast of North America
GROWTH TYPE Perennial shrub that can climb or lean on other shrubs
HARDINESS ZONES 9-10
FLOWER COLOR Rose-red, tubular, 1-inch miniature snapdragon flowers clustered around tips of branches
HEIGHT 3 to 5 feet, sprawling to the same width
BLOOMING PERIOD Spring, but intermittent all year
HOW TO GROW Sun or light shade; soils non-specific as long as drainage is adequate. Sensitive to heavy frosts. Control sprawling with winter pruning.
CULTIVARS AND RELATED SPECIES 'Firecracker' is a cultivated form that is more compact with bright red flowers.

JUSTICIA
Justicia spicigera

NATIVE HABITAT Mexico and Central America
GROWTH TYPE Perennial shrub

HARDINESS ZONES 9-10
FLOWER COLOR Orange whorls of 1½-inch tubular flowers at ends of protruding branches
HEIGHT 6 to 8 feet
BLOOMING PERIOD All year
HOW TO GROW Full sun or light shade in sandy or loamy fertile soils. Drought-tolerant; no water needed during dry season.
CULTIVARS AND RELATED SPECIES *J. brandegeana*, also known as shrimp plant, is an evergreen shrub with 3-inch spikes of white tubular flowers protruding from coppery bronze, overlapping bracts; blooms all year; sensitive to frost and requires regular watering. *J. californica*, chuparosa or California belperone, is a deciduous, low, gray-green, spreading shrub 2 to 5 feet high; spring blooms of bright red, clustered 1½-inch tubular flowers; needs no dry-season water; sensitive to freeze but will regenerate in spring.

LUPINE
Lupinus species

NATIVE HABITAT Numerous species prominent in a variety of habitats throughout the western U.S. with more than 80 species native to California, Oregon, Washington, and Alaska
GROWTH TYPE Annual or perennial herb or shrub
HARDINESS ZONES 4-10
FLOWER COLOR Mostly blue or

Lupinus arcticus

purple, some yellow or white, with flowers of five petals (an upper banner, two wings at sides, and two below joined as a keel) clustered at ends of short branches
HEIGHT Ranges from flat ground cover of 3 to 4 inches to bushes of 2 to 5 feet. Most species range from 6 to 18 inches in height.
BLOOMING PERIOD Spring, summer, and fall
HOW TO GROW Most lupines thrive in dry, sunny areas with well-drained soils. A few, such as the bush lupines, tolerate filtered shade and some dampness.
CULTIVARS AND RELATED SPECIES Some popular lupines include: *L. breweri*, brewer lupine, grows to 9

inches in gray-green leafy mats; flower clusters dense to 2 inches long with ¼-inch flowers with blue banner and white center; summer blooming; thrives on dry, stony slopes. *L. albifrons*, bush lupine, features leaves that are silvery and silky; flower clusters 3- to 12-inches long and flowers to ⅓ inch; petals blue to red-purple; banner white- or yellow-centered; spring bloom; sun or shade. *L. nootkantensis* and *L. arcticus* attract Rufous Hummingbirds in southeastern Alaska.

MONKEYFLOWER
Mimulus cardinalis

NATIVE HABITAT Along streams and in moist places throughout the western U.S.
GROWTH TYPE Herbaceous perennial often grown as an annual
HARDINESS ZONES 7-9
FLOWER COLOR Bright orange-red, 1-inch flowers with a funnel form widening to lobed upper and lower lips, often described as resembling a monkey face
HEIGHT 1 to 3 feet
BLOOMING PERIOD Spring and summer
HOW TO GROW Full sun or partial shade and damp conditions
CULTIVARS AND RELATED SPECIES *M. guttatus*, yellow monkeyflower, is also an inhabitant of streamside or moist locations; spreading foliage to about 1 foot with yellow flowers resembling *M. cardinalis*.

M. aurantiacus, sticky monkeyflower or bush monkeyflower, is a perennial shrub native to coastal sage scrub and foothills throughout California with 1-inch flowers, usually orange but ranging from red to pink and yellow; blooms spring, summer, and fall; drought-resistant but needs occasional water and some pruning to preserve lush bright green foliage and prevent it from becoming woody.

ORANGE LARKSPUR
Delphinium nudicaule

NATIVE HABITAT Northern California and southwestern Oregon
GROWTH TYPE Herbaceous perennial, often treated as annual
HARDINESS ZONES 8-9
FLOWER COLOR Red with long spurs, about ¾-inch long; very few per plant
HEIGHT Slender plants of 1 to 3 feet
BLOOMING PERIOD Summer
HOW TO GROW Sow seeds in spring in containers or in garden in full or filtered sun; needs rich, porous soil and periodic fertilizing. No water in late summer. Thrives in rock gardens or woodlands.
CULTIVARS AND RELATED SPECIES *Delphinium cardinale*, scarlet larkspur, has erect stems 3- to 6-feet tall and produces 1-inch, scarlet and yellow flowers; sow seed early for spring blooms.

Left: *Mimulus cardinalis*. Right: *Salvia elegans*

PINEAPPLE SAGE, RED SAGE
Salvia elegans (S. rutilans)

NATIVE HABITAT Mexico and Guatemala
GROWTH TYPE Perennial herb
HARDINESS ZONES 5 to 10
FLOWER COLOR Scarlet-red, slender, tubular flowers
HEIGHT To 5 feet and as wide
BLOOMING PERIOD Spring to fall, depending upon climate
HOW TO GROW Full sun or part shade, well-drained soils; is sensitive to frost. Can be grown from cuttings; prune regularly.
CULTIVARS AND RELATED SPECIES *S. splendens*, scarlet sage, is an annual, sturdy plant that grows 1 to 3 feet tall, topped with dense spikes of scarlet-red flowers blooming summer and fall. *S. spathacea*, hummingbird sage, a robust perennial, has large, aromatic leaves and whorls of magenta flowers. It grows best in full or filtered sun with some water. Many species of sage attract hummingbirds and thrive in the arid West, although they vary in height, shape, and flower color.

REHMANNIA, CHINESE FOXGLOVE
Rehmannia elata

NATIVE HABITAT China
GROWTH TYPE Evergreen shrub
HARDINESS ZONES 6-9

PACIFIC COAST

FLOWER COLOR Flowers resemble foxglove and range from rose to purple with red-dotted yellow throats.
HEIGHT 2 to 3 feet
BLOOMING PERIOD Long blooming period from April through November
HOW TO GROW This species is easy to grow and spreads from underground roots; plant in rich soil. Will grow in sun but thrives with some shade. Is deciduous in colder climates.
CULTIVARS AND RELATED SPECIES *R. glutinosa* differs from *R. elata* in having glandular hairs on its leaves.

Mimulus aurantiacus

STICKY MONKEYFLOWER, BUSH MONKEYFLOWER
Mimulus aurantiacus

NATIVE HABITAT Coastal sage scrub and foothills throughout California
GROWTH TYPE Perennial shrub
HARDINESS ZONES 9-10
FLOWER COLOR 1-inch flowers usually orange, but range from red to pink and yellow; funnel-form widening to lobed upper and lower lips. Generally one flower per leaf at ends of stems.
HEIGHT 4 feet
BLOOMING PERIOD Spring, summer, and fall
HOW TO GROW Drought-resistant but needs occasional water and some pruning to preserve lush, bright green foliage and to prevent plant from becoming woody.
CULTIVARS AND RELATED SPECIES *M. longiflorus*, southern bush monkeyflower, is similar to *M. aurantiacus*, but flowers mostly longer than 2 inches and ½ inch wide, pinkish yellow; native to Southern California. *M. puniceus*, red bush monkeyflower, is a shrub; flowers similar to other monkeyflowers in all hues of red to orange.

SCARLET MONARDELLA
Madronella macrantha

NATIVE HABITAT Dry slopes of the western U.S.
GROWTH TYPE Deciduous shrub

HARDINESS ZONES 7-9
FLOWER COLOR Large, red-orange whorls of flowers with purplish bracts, irresistible to hummingbirds
HEIGHT 2 to 3 feet
BLOOMING PERIOD Mid- to late summer
HOW TO GROW Requires very well-drained soils or else becomes difficult to grow; however, it is a good container plant when gravel is added to the soil mix.

SCARLET LARKSPUR
Delphinium cardinale

NATIVE HABITAT California coastal mountains south of Monterey
GROWTH TYPE Herbaceous perennial sometimes treated as annual; robust with tall stems from woody roots
HARDINESS ZONES 8-9
FLOWER COLOR Red with narrow yellow lobes
HEIGHT 3 to 6 feet
BLOOMING PERIOD Late spring, early summer
HOW TO GROW Grows in full or filtered sun in rich, alkaline soils. Fertilize regularly; no water necessary in late summer. Sow seed early for spring blooms.
CULTIVARS AND RELATED SPECIES *Delphinium nudicaule*, orange larkspur is a slender plant 1 to 3 feet tall; flowers ¾-inch long, red with long spurs; very few per plant.

TWINBERRY
Lonicera involucrata

NATIVE HABITAT Western forest belts in moist shady areas and along streams
GROWTH TYPE Herbaceous shrubby vine
HARDINESS ZONES 6-9
FLOWER COLOR Yellow to yellow-orange with reddish bracts at base, cylindrical trumpet-shaped with five lobes at end; ½ inch in pairs on stalk with leaves
HEIGHT 2 to 3 feet
BLOOMING PERIOD Spring, summer
HOW TO GROW Full sun to partial shade; water regularly as it needs lots of moisture; thrives in cooler climates or higher elevations.
CULTIVARS AND RELATED SPECIES *L. hispidula*, western honeysuckle, is a woody vine native to California and usually grown for berries; full sun or partial shade; water regularly; pink flowers are not flashy, but hummingbirds find them; summer blooms. *L. interrupta*, chaparral honeysuckle, is a climbing evergreen vine with woody trunk with ¾-inch elliptical leaves; red five-lobed tubular flowers on 2- to 5-inch spikes; blooms spring to summer; native to dry slopes. Fairly drought-tolerant; plant in sandy or loamy well-drained soils.

PACIFIC COAST

WESTERN COLUMBINE
Aquilegia formosa

NATIVE HABITAT Meadows and damp areas of western mountains, Pacific Northwest, and Alaska
GROWTH TYPE Herbaceous annual; erect stems from low-growing, 1½-foot plant
HARDINESS ZONES 6-9
FLOWER COLOR Scarlet-red or orange backward-projecting petals with contrasting yellow sepals and protruding stamens. Flowers are erect or nodding.
HEIGHT 2 to 3 feet
BLOOMING PERIOD Spring to summer
HOW TO GROW Hardy, and will tolerate filtered shade, although will thrive in full sun, especially along coast or in mountains if planted in moist, rich soils.
CULTIVARS AND RELATED SPECIES Native and hybridized

MORE HUMMINGBIRD PLANTS FOR THE PACIFIC COAST

SHRUBS
HUMMINGBIRD FERN *Grevillea* 'Canberra'—An evergreen shrub with bright green, needle-like leaves, grows to 8 feet with clusters of small red flowers blooming in spring, native to Australia; Zones 6-9.
MANZANITA *Archtostaphylos* species—Numerous species of evergreen shrubs ranging from tall shrubs to prostrate ground cover, all with red bark and white, waxy, bell-shaped flowers; Zones vary by species.
MEXICAN BUSH SAGE *Salvia leucantha*—This Mexican native has long, slender, velvety purple or deep rose spikes with small white flowers. Plant in full sun; tolerates drought; prune periodically to prevent it from becoming woody; Zones 9-10.
RED SAGE *Salvia greggii*—Erect shrub, 3 to 4 feet; flowers late spring through fall; Zones 6-10.
TREE TOBACCO *Nicotiana glauca* and *N. alata*—*N. glauca* is shrubby or tree-like, growing to 20 feet and producing tubular yellow flowers; *N. alata* is a 2- to 3-foot shrub with tubular white flowers; Zones 7-9.

VINES
CAPE HONEYSUCKLE *Tecomaria capensis*—Climbing vine with yellow and white fragrant flowers; native to South Africa; Zones 6-9.
CHINESE LANTERN *Abutilon* x *hybridum*—Native to South Ameri-

columbine flowers range from 1½ to 3 inches with a variety of color combinations, including white, yellow, blues, and purples in addition to the red-orange and yellow combinations of *A. formosa* and *A. canadensis*. Plants range from 2 to 4 feet tall. Other species include: *A. brevistyla* (Alaska and mountain West) and *A. canadensis*, American columbine (rocky slopes and alkaline soils).

Right: *Aquilegia formosa*

ca, also called flowering maple because of broad, maple-like leaves; drooping bell-like flowers in red, pink, and yellow; Zones 6-9.
TRUMPET CREEPER *Campsis radicans*—Deciduous vine with large orange or red flaring tubular flowers; Zones 5-9.

PERENNIALS AND ANNUALS
BEE BALM *Monarda didyma*—Bushy with long, aromatic leaves and clusters of long, tubed, scarlet flowers; all zones.
BEE PLANT *Scrophularia californica*—Large perennial with tall stalks of tiny maroon flowers; Zones 7-9.
BLEEDING HEART *Dicentra spectabilis*—Graceful but short-lived perennial with fern-like foliage and rows of small, heart-shaped, pink, rose, or white flowers on leafless stems; Zones 6-9.
CORAL BELL OR ALUM ROOT *Heuchera sanguinea*—Evergreen growing 15- to 30-inches tall with compact clumps of roundish leaves clustered near ground and stalks of crimson or red bell-shaped flowers; all zones.
RED HOT POKER *Kniphofia uvaria*—Spikes of orange and yellow flowers, grows to 3 feet, native of South Africa; Zones 5-9.
SCARLET GILIA *Ipomopsis aggregata*—Narrow, erect single stems to 2½ feet with striking tubular, fanning red flowers about 1 inch in length in long, narrow clusters; Zones 4-7.

PACIFIC COAST

NURSERY SOURCES

NORTHEAST AND MIDWEST

BERGESON NURSERY
4177 County Hwy 1
Fertile, MN 56540
(218) 945-6988
No mail order

KURT BLUEMEL, INC.
2740 Greene Lane
Baldwin, MD 21013
$3 catalog

CARROLL GARDENS, INC.
444 East Main St.
Westminster, MD 21157-5540
(410) 876-7336

**WILD EARTH NATIVE
PLANT NURSERY**
P.O. Box 7258
Freehold, NJ 07728
(732) 308-9777
$2 catalog

SOUTHEAST

APPALACHEE NATIVE NURSERY
Route 3, Box 156
Monticello, FL 32344
(850) 997-8976

GREEN IMAGES
1333 Taylor Creek Rd.
Christmas, FL 32709
(407) 568-1333

THE NATIVES, INC.
P.O. Box 946
Davenport, FL 33836
(941) 422-6664

SOUTHWEST

PLANTS FOR THE SOUTHWEST
Agua Fria
Rte. 6 Box 11A
Santa Fe, NM 87501
(505) 438-8888

GREAT BASIN NATIVES
Box 114
Holden, UT 84636
(435) 795-2303

HIGH COUNTRY GARDENS
2902 Rufina St
Santa Fe, NM 87505-2929
(800) 925-9387

WILD SEED
P.O. Box 27751
Tempe, AZ 85285
(602) 276-3536
Free catalog

PACIFIC COAST

CALIFORNIA FLORA NURSERY
P.O. Box 3
Fulton, CA 95439
(707) 528-8813
No mail order. Native plants only

CORNFLOWER FARMS
P.O. Box 896
896 Elk Grove, CA 95759
(916) 689-1015

SOURCE DIRECTORIES

**ANDERSEN HORTICULTURAL
LIBRARY'S SOURCE LIST OF
PLANTS AND SEEDS**
Minnesota Landscape Arboretum
3675 Arboretum Dr., Box 39
Chanhassen, MN 55317-0039
(612) 443-2440

HORTUS NORTHWEST
9450 S.W. Comerce Circle #32
Wilsonville, OR 97070
(503) 570-0859

**NEW ENGLAND WILD
FLOWER SOCIETY**
Garden in the Woods
180 Hemenway Road
Framingham, MA 01701-0269
(508) 877-7630

**ASSOCIATION OF FLORIDA
NATIVE NURSERIES**
P.O. Box 434
Melrose, FL 32666
(800) 293-5413
www.afnn.org

**NURSERY SOURCES FOR
CALIFORNIA NATIVE PLANTS**
(Pub# DMGOFR 90-04; $10)
Dept. of Conservation
Division of Mines and Geology
Library
801 K Street, Mailstation 14-34
Sacramento, CA 95814-3532
(916) 445-5716

**LADY BIRD JOHNSON
WILDFLOWER CENTER**
4801 LaCrosse Blvd.
Austin, TX 78739
(512) 929-3600

FOR MORE INFORMATION

A Book of Salvias: Sages for Every Garden, Clebsch, Betsy, 1997. Portland, Oregon: Timber Press

Attracting Birds to Southern Gardens, Pope, Thomas, Neil Odenwald, and Charles Fryling, Jr., 1993. Dallas, Texas: Taylor Publishing Company

Bird Gardens, Kress, Stephen W. (ed.), 1998. Brooklyn, New York: Brooklyn Botanic Garden

Gardening with Native Plants of the South, Wasowski, Sally and Andy, 1994. Dallas, Texas: Taylor Publishing Company

How to Attract Hummingbirds and Butterflies, Arbuckle, Nancy and Cedric Crocker, (eds.), 1991. San Ramon, California: Ortho Books

Hummingbird Gardens, Newfield, Nancy L. and Barbara Nielson, 1996. Shelburne, Vermont: Chapters' Publishing, Ltd.

Songbirds in Your Garden, Terres, John K, 1994. Chapel Hill, North Carolina: Algonquin Books

The Audubon Society Bird Garden, Kress, Stephen W., 1995. New York: Dorling Kindersley

The Birds of North America, Poole, Alan and Frank Gill (eds.) The Academy of Natural Sciences, Philadelphia and the American Ornithologists' Union, Washington, D.C.

The Hummingbird Book, Stokes, Donald and Lillian, 1989. Boston: Little Brown and Co.

The Hummingbirds of North America, Johnsgard, Paul A., 2nd ed., 1997. Washington D.C.: Smithsonian Institution Press

The Southern Living Garden Book: The Complete Encyclopedia of More Than 5,000 Southern Plants, 1998. Birmingham, Alabama: Oxmoor House Book Division of Southern Progress Corporation

Anna's Hummingbird

ORGANIZATIONS

For further information about attracting hummingbirds and other backyard wildlife, contact the following groups:

CORNELL LABORATORY OF ORNITHOLOGY
159 Sapsucker Woods Road
Ithaca, NY 14850

NATIONAL AUDUBON SOCIETY
700 Broadway
New York, NY 10003

NATIONAL WILDLIFE FEDERATION
8925 Leesburg Pike
Vienna, VA 22184

CONTRIBUTORS

JESSE GRANTHAM is the Executive Director of the Mississippi State Office of the National Audubon Society. He has extensive experience in horticulture, habitat restoration, and wildlife management. He initiated a very successful partnership between Monrovia Nursery and Audubon called "Audubon Habitats," which promotes landscaping with native plants. He writes and lectures throughout the country on gardening for wildlife.

BETH HUNING is Director of Education for the National Audubon Society in California. She has directed the education and wildlife conservation programs at the 900-acre waterbird sanctuary and environmental education center for Audubon's Richardson Bay Audubon Center and Sanctuary on San Francisco Bay, where she coordinated the development of wildlife habitat programs and demonstration gardens, including a model hummingbird garden.

STEPHEN W. KRESS is Vice-President for Bird Conservation of the National Audubon Society and Director of the Society's Seabird Restoration Program. He teaches ornithology classes at the Audubon Camp in Maine and for the Cornell Laboratory of Ornithology. Stephen guest-edited the Brooklyn Botanic Garden handbook *Bird Gardens* (1998). He is author of *The Audubon Society Bird Garden, The Audubon Society Birder's Handbook*, the *Golden Guide Bird Life*, and other publications on birds and their management.

LYNN HASSLER KAUFMAN has been birdwatching, gardening, and studying plants for more than 25 years. She is Vice-President of the Arizona Native Plant Society and a staff member of the Tucson Botanical Gardens. She is an experienced leader of bird and wildflower trips. She is a columnist for *Bird Watcher's Digest* and the author of the "Deserts" volume in the Peterson Coloring Book Series published by Houghton Mifflin, and has written widely about gardening.

CREDITS

ILLUSTRATIONS

All illustrations by
STEVE BUCHANAN

PHOTOS

**DONALD WAITE/
CORNELL LABORATORY OF
ORNITHOLOGY,** cover

CHARLES MANN, pages 2, 42,
44, 63, 66, 72, 74, 76, 78 top, 85,
89, 92, 95 left

R. & N. BOWERS/VIREO,
page 4

B. RANDALL/VIREO, page 7

D. TRUE/VIREO, pages 9, 33
bottom

R. & S. DAY/VIREO, page 10

C.A. FOGLE/VIREO, page 12

J. DUNNING/VIREO, pages 32,
33 top

DAVID CAVAGNARO, pages 35,
41, 43, 51, 52, 55, 57, 58, 61, 62,
65, 67, 68, 77, 78 bottom, 83, 86,
88, 90, 91, 95 right, 99

**STEVEN PANTLE/
CORNELL LABORATORY OF
ORNITHOLOGY,** page 45

**ISIDOR JEKLIN/
CORNELL LABORATORY OF
ORNITHOLOGY,** page 47

H.P. SMITH/VIREO, page 48

ALAN & LINDA DETRICK, pages
50, 54

SUSAN M. GLASCOCK, pages
53, 60

JERRY PAVIA, pages 82, 93, 96

**PATRICIA MEACHAM/
CORNELL LABORATORY OF
ORNITHOLOGY,** page 103

USDA HARDINESS ZONE MAP

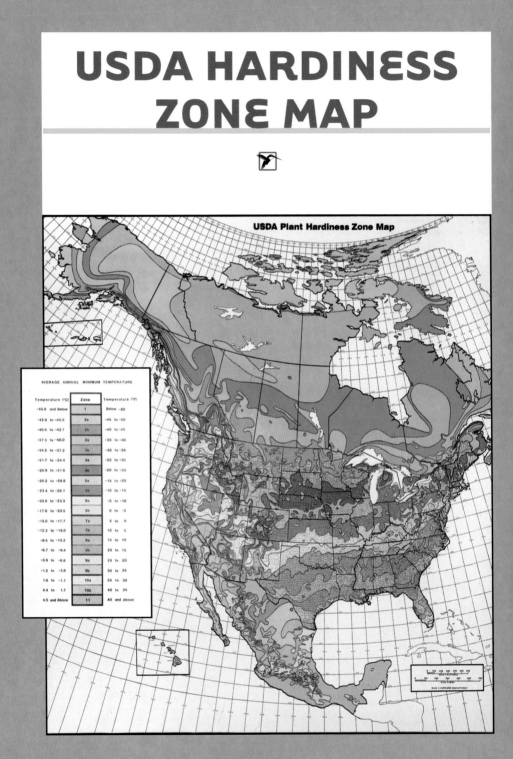

USDA Plant Hardiness Zone Map

AVERAGE ANNUAL MINIMUM TEMPERATURE

Temperature (°C)	Zone	Temperature (°F)
-45.6 and Below	1	Below -50
-42.8 to -45.5	2a	-45 to -50
-40.0 to -42.7	2b	-40 to -45
-37.3 to -40.0	3a	-35 to -40
-34.5 to -37.2	3b	-30 to -35
-31.7 to -34.4	4a	-25 to -30
-28.9 to -31.6	4b	-20 to -25
-26.2 to -28.8	5a	-15 to -20
-23.4 to -26.1	5b	-10 to -15
-20.6 to -23.3	6a	-5 to -10
-17.8 to -20.5	6b	0 to -5
-15.0 to -17.7	7a	5 to 0
-12.3 to -15.0	7b	10 to 5
-9.5 to -12.2	8a	15 to 10
-6.7 to -9.4	8b	20 to 15
-3.9 to -6.6	9a	25 to 20
-1.2 to -3.8	9b	30 to 25
1.6 to -1.1	10a	35 to 30
4.4 to 1.7	10b	40 to 35
4.5 and Above	11	40 and Above

INDEX

BROOKLYN BOTANIC GARDEN

MORE

BOOKS ON

GARDENING

FOR WILDLIFE